Cinema's Frontline

War Films from Silent Era to the Modern Day

by Cameron Jameson

Formatted, Converted, and Distributed by eBookIt.com
http://www.eBookIt.com

ISBN-13: 9781456641818 (paperback)
ISBN-13: 9781456641801 (ebook)
ISBN-13: 9781456641825 (audiobook)

Dear Esteemed Reader,

Thank you immensely for choosing this book to join your collection. We imagine that you've already embarked on an exploration of ideas within these pages, and we couldn't be happier about it!

Now, if you find yourself chuckling, pondering, or even debating with the words in front of you, we'd absolutely love to hear about it. If you can spare a few moments to pen down your thoughts in a review, we would be as delighted as a dictionary on a spelling bee!

An Amazon review would be excellent - but hey, we're far from picky. Whether it's a scribble on the back of a grocery list, a tweet, or even a message in a bottle (though that might take a while to reach us), your feedback is gold.

Writing a review might not be as fun as a spontaneous dance-off, but we promise it'll bring grins to our faces, warmth to our hearts, and incredibly valuable insights to future readers.

With Gratitude,

Bo Bennett, PhD
Publisher
Archieboy Holdings, LLC.

Table of Contents

Introduction

War films, an illustrious genre steeped in profound narratives and riveting action sequences, have intrigued audiences all over the world. Their capacity to incite reflection, provoke dialogue, and stimulate empathy is unrivaled. Yet, how did these epic battle sequences erupt from silver screens, redrawing historical battles and modern armed conflicts alike? This book will lift the curtain on the mesmerizing art of war filmmaking, unraveling its transformation from its humble inception to its current sophisticated form, and analyzing its deep-seated influence on society. Today, as we delve into this exciting odyssey, we aren't merely spectators; we are explorers embarking on a quest to unravel the manifestation of war on screen. Along the way, we will expose the intricacies of war cinema, its evolution and impacts, and thereby comprehend how it became such a distinguished part of our culture. Let's march forth into the trenches, to feel the spirit, the sacrifices, and the saga that war cinemas have offered us.

The Importance of War Films

The genre of war films holds diverse significance in the annals of cinema history. Just as the ripple of a stone cast into still waters extends its influence far and wide, the impact of war films permeates cultural boundaries, impacts societal views, and catalyzes changes within the film industry itself.

War films, at their heart, are more than simple representations of historical battles and military strategies. They are a canvas painted with the hues of human emotions, struggles, and triumphs. They serve as a reflection of the times they depict, embodying the prevalent societal views, political mindset, and cultural sensitivities. In that sense, war films can be seen as time capsules, capturing the essence of eras passed and making them accessible to future generations.

Stories of war evoke raw emotions - pain, sorrow, triumph, and a whole gamut of sentiments that deeply resonate with audiences. These films uniquely present a narrative of courage that celebrates human perseverance in the face of adversity. They spotlight people from all walks of life exhibiting heroism and bravery that might otherwise have remained unsung. Through this, war films empower us as viewers, glorifying ordinary individuals who rise to the occasion during extraordinary times.

When it comes to understanding the socio-political climate of an era, war films prove to be valuable tools. They may be fiction, but their setting, their conflicts, and their resolutions are derived from reality. As such, war films have the ability to define public perception about specific historical events and times, and in some cases, carry the power to rewrite narrative discourse altogether.

Consider, for instance, the films set during the World War II era. These films didn't just glorify the war effort or present heroic deeds. They also captured the essence of life during the war, the decisions average individuals were forced to make, the role of women, minorities, and other key societal aspects. Through their narratives, these films managed to comment on, critique, and at times, alter the perceptions associated with such periods.

War films have also proven essential to the growth of the film industry, pushing its boundaries and accelerating technological advancements. The battlefield allows for the creation of spectacular visuals and demands the exploration of novel filmmaking techniques. War films have prompted significant transformations in film techniques, demanding everything from enhanced special effects, prop and set designs, to cinematic narrative styles.

These films have also provided a platform for filmmakers to challenge conventional storytelling methods, enabling them to delve deeper into the human psyche, explore moral complexities, and interpret historical facts in compelling ways. They have redefined the norms of narrative cinema, making space for the audience to question, debate, and challenge their perception of concepts such as patriotism, extremism, sacrifice, and the very nature of war itself.

War films, through their realistic representations of battlefield chaos, have paved the way for incredibly immersive sound design. They demand authenticity in depiction, pushing sound designers to innovate ways to recreate the sensations of warfare. Such films have laid the groundwork for the immersive soundscapes we experience in contemporary cinema.

A spotlight must also be shone on the pivotal role that war films have played in providing representation and voice to veterans. They're able to encapsulate and convey the physical and psychological struggles that soldiers endure during and after combat. These films create a heightened public awareness of soldiers' traumas and struggles, prompting much-needed conversations about veterans' care and support.

War films also hold immense educational value, offering the audience a perspective into the intricacies of historical events. They bring forth the human narratives that textbooks often fail to accommodate. This ability to humanize history makes war films an irreplaceable asset to the field of education.

Over time, war films have strived to tell inclusive stories, shedding light on the experiences of women and minorities. By doing so, they've instigated much-needed discourse on representation and diversity in cinema, and have contributed to the gradual, but significant, evolution of film narratives.

However, it's also crucial to consider the ethical issues associated with war filmmaking. Striking a balance between authenticity, sensitivity, and entertainment value poses challenges that filmmakers must constantly navigate. This adds yet another layer to their significance, as war films often motivate discussions about the very ethics of filmmaking.

To sum it up, war films are far more than simple entertainments - they are essential conduits of education, evokers of emotion, ignitors of conversation, and catalysts for progress within the film industry. Their importance lies not just in the stories they tell, but the lasting impact they leave behind on society, culture, and cinema.

Let's now venture forth, delving into the intricacies of the genre, tracing its birth, evolution, and transformation through the chapters that follow. Films, like war, can be transformative. They have the ability to change the viewer and the society they're part of. And perhaps that makes understanding the importance of war films all the more essential.

Objectives of the Book

The essential aim of this book is to delve into the historical journey of war films, examining their evolution through different eras, and exploring their profound impact on society. We aim to provide readers with an in-depth understanding of war films' importance, including the emotions, perspectives, and narratives they convey about wars.

Studying the inception of the genre in the era of silent film, we will dissect the rudimentary components that, over time, underpinned the genre's success. From scripting to directing — all aspects that have enabled cinematic battles — this book provides a comprehensive educational journey for the reader. Furthermore, it intends to offer an exploration of culture's role in shaping war films and vice versa.

As we venture into the Golden Age and World War II cinema, the aim is to analyze Hollywood's portrayal of global conflict, throwing light on the sensed patriotism, propaganda, and art involved. We will dissect how the cinematic angle on the world wars influenced society's aftermath, shaping post-war perception, and understanding.

When analyzing the portrayal of the Cold War on screen, we intend to demonstrate how the invisible battle has been filmed, how cultural anxiety has been depicted, and how the era added innovative chapters to the film-making industry.

Through the lens of the Vietnam War, we aim to expound on how war movies took a revolutionary turn, infusing raw emotions and reality into their depiction. Here, we will examine the impact of the protest movement on the film industry, spotlighting remarkable directors and films from this era.

As we analyze modern warfare in film, our intention is to observe how technological advancements have significantly changed war film production and conveyance. We'll talk about society's fluctuating views on modern conflicts and take note of the prominent modern war films and their sub-genres.

By examining the influence of war films on veterans, we intend to illustrate the cinematic representation of soldiers and how it can potentially aid their healing process. This objective echoes the book's aim to make a chronological narration of the evolution of war films a reflective voyage ripe with enlightening insights.

Understanding the role of women and minorities in such films resonates with our ambition to analyze changing roles, breakthrough films, characters, and social commentary conveyed through these movies. This objective emphasizes our intent to go beyond mere storytelling analysis and delve into deeper societal discussions through cinema.

While following the journey of war films, we also aim to unmask the ethical side of war filmmaking, grappling with balancing art and sensitivity. We will explore the controversies, criticism, and ethical debates revolving around this genre, reflecting on the decisions makers must face.

Intriguingly, the book aspires to discuss war films' future, emerging technologies, techniques, and the new perspectives brought on by the new conflicts. It views the future of war films as a continually evolving domain, influenced by globalization and an ever-changing socio-political landscape.

Lastly, we hope to offer the readers a reflective look at cinema's frontline, aiming to explore the ongoing impact and legacy of war films. By discussing the intersection of art and reality, we desire to underline the genre's potential to echo, provoke, and even predict societal trends and discourses, thereby playing a vital role in shaping public perceptions of war.

In sum, the primary objective of this book is to provide readers with an engaging and informative chronicle of war films, touching on their genesis, evolution, and impact. We hope that this deep dive into the genre will not only entertain but also enlighten readers about the myriad ways in which war films embody, express, and influence our perceptions of war, our society, and our collective history.

We firmly believe that irrespective of whether you are a film student, a war movie enthusiast, or even a casual reader with an interest in how wars are portrayed in film, this book will serve as an illuminating, immersive, and insightful read, keeping you engaged with its interlacing of cinema, history, culture, and society. Let's together embark on this voyage into the remarkable world of war cinema!

Chapter 1: First Look into War Films

War films, as a cinematic exploration, undertake a formidable task: encapsulating the raw essence of humanity's most devastating and transformative calamities. The birth of this genre introduced a novel form of storytelling, forever reshaping the cinematic landscape. This initial leap drew audiences to the silver screen as though it were a battlefield—without the bloodshed, yet with the emotional turmoil intact. With the magic of filmmaking, the indescribable pain, unfathomable bravery, and universal lessons at war's heart were distilled into a shared narrative experience accessible to all. Film, inherently a collective pastime, amplified the reach of war's narratives in unique ways, forging connections and inciting dialogues across boundaries of geography and time. However, it's not just the depiction of war itself that distinguished this emerging genre; its profound cultural impact proved to be yet another contributing factor to its immense relevance. Through often stark portrayals of heroism and loss, war films not only mirrored society's attitudes and anxieties but also questioned, critiqued, and, in some instances, reshaped those very beliefs. This chapter provides a sweeping exploration into the genesis of the genre, the analogies drawn between cinema and warfare, and an overarching view of war films' cultural influence. It offers a captivating narrative intertwining film history and societal evolution while setting the stage for a detailed exploration of war films through various epochs.

Birth of the Genre

In the wide and comprehensive spectrum of the film industry, the birth of the war genre marked a turning point. It's a genre that has been in existence almost as long as movies themselves, originating from the late 1890s. It was a period when cinema was a consuming novelty, eagerly welcomed by a public eager to be transported to different realities, and war offered one of the most intense and significant of those realities.

This genre did not emerge out of the blue, though. There was a mixture of historical events, technological advancements, and societal changes that paved the way for it. The first usage of moving pictures to capture war occurred during the Spanish-American War in 1898, with the staged but convincing "Tearing Down the Spanish Flag" by J. Stuart Blackton.

The next significant milestone in the inception of the war genre was the 1915 film "The Birth of a Nation" by D.W. Griffith. Despite controversial themes and offensive depictions of various races, this film was groundbreaking in its early use of cinematic techniques such as cross-cutting and close-ups, and for depicting the Civil War's devastating impact.

Subsequently, World War I played an instrumental role in the early evolution of war films. Due to the cataclysmic scale of the war, films emerging from this era, such as Charlie Chaplin's "Shoulder Arms" (1918) and Abel Gance's "J'Accuse" (1919), depicted the ghastly horrors of the front lines and the tragedies of those left at home, respectively.

In the 1920s and 30s, war films continued to grow in popularity. The development of sound cinema in the late

1920s added a new dimension to the war genre, with films like "All Quiet on the Western Front" (1930) adding the rattling sounds of machine gunfire and the haunting gasps of the dying soldiers, thus augmenting the audience's immersion into the reality of warfare.

The start of the Second World War in 1939 accelerated the evolution of the genre. Considering the massive scale and unprecedented consequences of the war, the genre evolved from merely showing events to becoming a platform for propagating ideas and sentiments. Hence, many films produced during this period, like "The Great Dictator," (1940) by Charlie Chaplin, utilized the war genre to make political statements and influence public opinion.

Post-WWII, the Cold War years formed the backdrop for another significant evolution of the genre, with films such as Stanley Kubrick's "Dr. Strangelove" (1964) offering satirical commentary on the absurdity of nuclear warfare.

This era also saw the birth of another key subgenre – the POW film. "The Great Escape" (1963), inspired by real-life events during World War II, was a classic example, highlighting the ordeals of captured military personnel.

As the world stepped into the heart-wrenching era of the Vietnam War, the war genre thoroughly evolved, reflecting the disillusionment and critique of the war that characterized society of the time. Films like "Apocalypse Now" (1979) and "Platoon" (1986) became defining examples of this era, portraying war in an unflinchingly harsh light, scaling new heights in realism and brutality.

In more recent times, war films have sought to tackle modern warfare and its related issues. From the sectarian conflicts of the Middle East, as seen in "The Hurt Locker"

(2008), to the ongoing war against terrorism in films such as "American Sniper" (2014), the war genre continues to adapt to the changing times and the shifting theaters of conflict.

Throughout this journey, the genre has remained attentive to the human experience. Be it reflecting the collective psyche of the soldier, exploring the complexities of survival amid chaos, or delving into the politics and power dynamics of war, these films foreground the people caught in the throes of strife.

One of the defining characteristics of the war genre has been its ability to freshen its scope continuously, shedding new light on old narratives, questioning established beliefs, and reconfiguring the viewing lens through which audiences perceive the concept of war.

Concurrently, war films emerged as profound tools for historical documentation. They provided an accessible and compelling means for successive generations to engage with the tumultuous periods of yesteryears, bridging the gap between past and present.

To conclude, the birth of the war genre was not a singular event but a continual evolution - a reflection of the ever-changing global landscape. As we delve deeper into this genre in the following chapters, we'll unearth its multifaceted nature, its impact on society, and its testament to the art of cinema. In essence, war films are not just about wars but an exploration of humanity under extreme stressing conditions, upholding a mirror to our civilization.

Cinema as a Battlefield

Having explored the birth of the war film genre, we find ourselves at the heart of the matter - Cinema as a Battlefield. We're not talking literally here, but viewing cinema as a battleground allows us delve into the core of war films. For it is not just on physical fields that battles are fought, but on the silver screens where stories of heroism, cruelty, bravery, and the sheer human will to survive are spun right before our eyes.

The cinema, as an impactful form of mass communication, serves as an influential platform in shaping and reflecting public opinion. In the context of war films, the unyielding power of cinema opens avenues to our understanding of the complexities and consequences of wars, and conflicts.

While a war unfolds across miles of no-man's land, its stories and implications seep into the universal consciousness via cinema. Be it the chaotic trenches of World War I, the mobilized armies of World War II, scorching jungles of Vietnam or the harsh desert landscapes of the Iraqi invasion, the cinema recreates these battlefields with compelling authenticity. Each frame is a canvas, painted with the stark realities of war, embodying the triumphs and despairs of those who live it.

War films use a myriad of cinematic techniques like the crash-zooms into a soldier's terrified eyes, a low-angle shot to depict an imposing figure of authority, or a slow pan across desolate ruins to capture the after-effects of a battle. They utilize the arsenal of film language, visual and auditory elements, to induce within us a vivid understanding and impactful experience. The tactile realism and the emotional verisimilitude that these films bring forth affect us in ways that the printed word or spoken narratives cannot hold a candle against.

But it's not just about replicating the aesthetics of war. These films reflect and scrutinize the ethical, moral, and societal consequences of warfare. Some films denote a heroic tale of triumph over adversity, showcasing a nation's strength or a soldier's heroics. In contrast, others treat war as bleak and harrowing, spotlighting the human cost and harsh realities of conflict.

Filmmakers, like any artist, bring their individual perspectives and nuances to this battleground. Some directors present a stark and unturnished portrayal of war, stripping it off any perceived glamour or heroism while others take an unwavering patriotic stance, glorifying their nation's might and heroics. Every director utilizes their unique storytelling style, their arsenal of cinematic techniques, to make a statement on war and its implications.

This cinematic portrayal of war, while crafting compelling narratives, also serves as a conduit for socio-political discourse. Through a film, an audience may be led to empathize with their fellow countrymen on the field, question their government's motives, or even shift the tide of public sentiment for or against the war. For instance, such films can serve as a powerful tool in critiquing or supporting warfare depending on the narrative lens, highlighting the power the cinema holds in shaping our understanding and opinions of conflict.

Moreover, war films extend beyond showcasing battlefield realities. They delve into the human aspect, showcasing the psyche of a soldier, the dignities and indignities of life during wartime, and the post-war repercussions. From the agonizing wait for orders to the struggle for sanity under constant threat, these films immerse us in the emotional battlefield inherent to war.

A closer look at war films and one discovers narratives that foreground the experiences of prisoners of war, homefront dynamics, or even the war correspondent's role. The aim is not to reinforce stereotypes but bring out the unseen dimensions of war into the public eye. It, in turn, prompts reflections and conversations about war and its deeper implications.

As filmmakers take us on this emotional rollercoaster, exploring multiple aspects of warfare, the potential cinematographic missteps are numerous. The presentation of war is a contentious issue and the filmmakers are caught in a catch-22 situation, where realism can be accused of sensationalism, and soft-pedaling can risk accusations of trivializing war's severity.

Ultimately, it's a tricky balance and a continual back-and-forth between the filmmaker's creative freedom and the duty towards presenting an authentic representation of war. This delicate negotiation forms the underlying tension in the cinematic portrayal of warfare and underscores the significance of cinema as a battleground.

By understanding 'Cinema as a Battlefield', we trace an essential evolution in the maturation of the war genre. The ability of films to tell stories that have the power to move us, challenge us, provoke thought, and ultimately lead to change can't be underestimated. They stand as a testament to cinema's capacity to reflect and influence society's perception of war.

As we move forward, we'll continue delving into the various eras of war films, navigating this battlefield of cinema, and understanding the impact they have had on our understanding and perceptions of war. From the silent era to modern warfare, the journey ahead promises to be as enlightening as it will be entertaining.

Cultural Impact and Overview

Looking back at the cinematographic arts, we can't ignore the genre that leaves a profound impact: war films. From the way they stimulate discussions about social, political, and ethical issues, to their influence on popular culture, these films have carved their mark into the fabric of our society.

Their innate ability to capture the essence of human resilience and the dark reality of wars has made them not merely pieces of entertainment, but cultural vestiges of human history. Through the lens of directors and storytellers, we view the duality of human nature exposed on the battlefield, and it's this peek that inevitably influences our perception of conflicts.

War films often echo the sentiments of their time. When discussing war films, one can't overlook their function as a social litmus test. By reflecting prevalent political climates, social norms, or cultural shifts, they hold a mirror to society, exposing often grim and stark realities.

Indeed, it's the archetypal function of art to imitate life, and cinema relentlessly embraces this grand responsibility. War films have solidified their standing within popular culture due to their perennial necessity; they stand as cinematic monuments to battles fought, victories savored, and losses mourned. The toil, courage, and sacrifice illuminated often send ripple effects across contemporary culture, fostering public conversation or catalyzing change.

Moreover, they serve as a handy documentation of our social history. Much like pearls on a string, they chronicle transformative periods of our collective past. Perhaps one of the most prominent examples is how the Hollywood Golden Age and WWII films were intimately tied together, showcasing not only the visible conflicts of the time but also the underlying ideological and cultural tensions.

War films also have an extraordinary ability to breed empathy and emotion, allowing the audience to walk in another's shoes. By portraying the fear, pain, courage, and resilience of combatants, these films carry the potential to evoke empathy and challenge our views on the sanctity of life, horrors of war, and the boleros of heroism. "Saving Private Ryan" left audiences shell-shocked with its brutally honest representation of WWII, while "Apocalypse Now" illustrates the intellectual and moral dilemmas associated with Vietnam.

In addition, they contribute significantly to national identity, subtly shaping our perception of patriotism, bravery, and sacrifice. The American film industry, in particular, used this genre as a tool to fortify public opinion and morale during times of war, often producing works defined by their unabashed patriotic fervor.

Furthermore, they offer a platform for political discourse and posturing. The stark representation of the enemy, the dichotomy of good and evil, justice versus injustice, and heroism against cowardice - all paint a vivid image of political agendas and beliefs. They challenge the audience, nudging them towards introspection on their own beliefs and ideologies.

War films have significantly influenced the fashion industry as well. Military-inspired clothing and accessories, such as bomber jackets, combat boots, and camo prints, have found their place in our wardrobes thanks to their popularity on the big screen.

More than just a cultural product, these films play an active role in shaping and influencing culture itself. The often grim themes have even made their way into our lexicon, with phrases such as "in the trenches," "on the front lines," and "no man's land" becoming ingrained idioms, their origins synonymous with the war genre.

Society, forever engaged in a dance with cinema, often finds itself taking cues from war films. Their portrayal of minorities, for instance, wields significant weight in reshaping outdated narratives and emerging symbols of inclusivity.

Let us not overlook the crucial element of how this genre has reshaped educational discourse. They serve as a veritable teaching tool, particularly for those less inclined towards traditional learning. War films have expanded discussions outside of the classrooms, engaging people in historical dialogue.

And lastly, there's an essential facet when it comes to war films: they harbor a collective memory of warfare—a cultural product that serves as a time capsule, capturing unique, defining moments in our shared history.

In essence, war films carry a much deeper impact beyond their runtime. With their unique blend of storytelling and reality, they permeate through different aspects of our culture, forging an essential link between cinema and society.

Chapter 2: The Silent Era of War Films

Transitioning from the genre's birth into the Silent Era, war films began to soberly mirror society's struggle and exploit the latent power of visual storytelling. The lack of spoken dialogue led to innovative storytelling techniques; directors became masters at utilizing basic film components—like lighting, camera angles, and shot transitions—as conduits of emotion and drama. Moreover, the absence of language barriers allowed silent war films to resonate globally, heightening their influence. Historical events echoed on screens, crafting societal reflections that allowed audiences to appreciate the gravitas of war. Pioneers of this era were tasked not just with conveying historical accuracy, but with conveying genuine emotions sans dialogue—challenging filmmakers to venture into uncharted territory. Films such as Abel Gance's 'J'accuse' and King Vidor's 'The Big Parade' became iconic, setting benchmarks for future war films. These silent spectacles were not merely passive renderings of valiant heroes and battles won, but intricate narratives examining the human condition in times of conflict. They elicited deep-seated fears and propagated national ideologies, shaping the framework for how society viewed both its past and its future.

Early Techniques and Storytelling

The dawn of the cinematic age saw the birth of numerous genres. Among these, the war film genre emerged with gusto, providing keen insights into the struggles and victories of conflict. Using initial techniques available, filmmakers embarked on a journey of storytelling that visually presented the grimness, the heroism, and the heart of war.

One of the earliest films to apply these techniques was "The Battle of San Juan Hill," a 1898 movie that depicted the Spanish-American War. Despite its short running time and limited resources, it was an attempt to capture the truth of battle. The movie used wide shots to illustrate the sheer enormity of war and show the charging soldiers, creating a sense of action and urgency that immediately transported the audience to the ground.

Subsequently, D.W. Griffith's 1915 epic film, "The Birth of a Nation," explored the dynamics of the Civil War and its aftermath. Despite its controversial themes, it revolutionized the way war was presented on screen. The film pioneered techniques such as camera motion, cross-cutting scenes and close-ups to enhance the dramatic intensity of the storyline, thus amplifying the emotional resonance for audiences.

Another cornerstone of early war film techniques was the use of practical effects to narrate the calamity of war. For instance, "All Quiet on the Western Front," created in 1930, faithfully illustrated the horrifying trenches of World War I. The filmmakers used explosives on set to simulate shell explosions and hand-crafted models to demonstrate the destruction of infrastructure.

The choice of set, costume, and props were crucial in creating an authentic representation of the time. The 1927 feature "Wings," used actual World War I aircrafts and shot scenes at real airfields. This emphasis on realism set the stage for future war films, which have strived to depict conflicts accurately and truthfully.

Often deemed as the first great film of sound, "All Quiet on the Western Front" showcased powerful audio techniques that helped in revolutionizing cinema. From the wailing sirens to the deafening boom of artillery fire, the film heightened its auditory experience, making the audience feel as though they too were on the front lines.

Concurrent to these dramatic advancements in visual storytelling, the silent era of war films brought forth a unique method of engaging the audience. Without sound, filmmakers leaned heavily on visual cues and title cards to convey intricate emotions and complex narratives. This reliance on visuals led to more expressive and evocative plaes, ultimately pushing the limits of physical acting.

The silent war film, "The Big Parade" (1925), is an inimitable example of how wordless performances, coupled with powerful imagery, managed to paint a vivid picture of the brutality of war. This emphasis on showing, rather than telling, led to an evolution in the audience's understanding and perception of conflict.

Apart from the devastating battlefield sequences, war films in this era also focused on the emotional toll that war took on the individuals involved. "The General" (1926), a silent comedy film set during the American Civil War, subtly consolidated the human aspect of war. It showcased the protagonist's resilience during distressing times, successfully humanizing the concept of 'soldier' for the audience.

The storytelling techniques used in these early films did not merely serve as dramatic reconstructions of war events. In essence, they served as a bridge, narrowing the gap between civilians and the armed forces. By highlighting the horrors of war and the bravery of the soldiers, these movies allowed viewers to grasp the cost of freedom and peace.

War films also played a critical role in communicating societal ideologies. These were showcased in "The Lost Battalion" (1919), depicting a group of American soldiers surrounded by German forces during World War I. The movie took great pains to depict the enemy as monstrous and formidable, subtly but unmistakably reflecting and shaping societal attitudes towards the conflict.

War has a story to tell. A story of victory, of defeat, of struggle, and of courage. Early filmmakers understood this and used their rudimentary techniques and storytelling prowess to bring these stories to life. They zoomed in on the reality of war, focusing on the grit and determination of soldiers, while also illustrating the harsh and devastating consequences of conflict.

The legacy of these early filmmakers is still evident today. Modern cinema has borrowed, evolved, and expanded upon these techniques, continually pushing the boundaries of war storytelling. Yet amidst the technological advancements and evolving aesthetics, the core essence of depicting the realities of conflict remains true to the pioneers of this genre.

Ultimately, the early techniques and storytelling methods used in war films served a purpose beyond entertainment. They became tools for reflection, conversation, and understanding, paving the way for a genre that continues to challenge us, move us, and inform our understanding of history and humanity.

Societal Reflections in Silent Films

The Silent Era of war films offers fascinating insights into societal perceptions of war and conflict during the times they were created. Nevertheless, silent war films went beyond simply documenting historical events. They became societal mirrors, reflecting the nuances, beliefs, and influences of societies that bore the brunt of battle.

A prime example of societal reflection is seen in "The Birth of a Nation" (1915) by D. W. Griffith. Amidst its depictions of the Civil War and Reconstruction Era, the film was simultaneously a cultural artifact holding a mirror up to the racial tensions in America. Though rightly criticized for its stark representation of racism, the film carries significant weight by shining a light on the societal attitudes of its time.

Another example, Cecil B. DeMille's "The Woman God Forgot" (1917), showcases the cultural fascination with explorations and conquests, aptly reflecting the era's imperialistic views. Through its narrative, we gain an understanding of prevalent attitudes around the world during an era of expanding colonial empires.

To the introspective observer, silent war films can be seen as powerful sociocultural time capsules, preserving the essence of societal perceptions during the time in which they were made. In "Wings" (1927) directed by William A. Wellman, the heroic representation of the American pilots reflects the surge of patriotism amidst the painful memories of World War I.

On the other hand, the silent war film "All Quiet on the Western Front" (1930), based on Erich Maria Remarque's novel, graphically reflects the horrors of war, a grim contrast from the romanticized notions widely propagated by society.

Many of these films displayed not only the heroism of soldiers but also the humanity that exists even amidst the harsh realities of war. This can be seen in "The Big Parade" (1925), which tenderly illustrates a mix of camaraderie, romance, and tragedy, thus shedding light on the multifaceted nature of human experiences during times of war.

As film technology advanced, so did the stories that were told. Filmmakers began highlighting, with greater accuracy, the experiences of those outside the battlefield. Films like 'The Crowd' (1928) and 'Broken Blossoms' (1919) encapsulate the societal impact war has on civilians, underlining the humanity caught in the crossfire of conflicts.

Films of this era also subtly reflected the societal belief systems and moral codes of their time. 'Hearts of the World' (1918) promulgates a moral high ground for the allies in World War I, while German-made 'The White Hell of Pitz Palu' (1929) showcases the German spirit of teamwork and sacrifice amidst extreme adversity.

Beyond their stimulation of emotions and patriotism, however, these films were also arenas for imparting specific societal values and ideologies. As tools of propaganda, movies like 'The Kaiser, Beast of Berlin' (1918), mirrored societies at war, shaping national identities and focusing public sentiment against the perceived enemy.

The societal reflections in silent films often extended their reach into the political sphere as well. Films such as "October: Ten Days that Shook the World" (1928) used the muted language of cinema to trumpet political messages, investing great effort into immortalizing the revolutionary spirit of its time.

While the societal reflections in silent films often stemmed from calculated decisions by filmmakers, the films themselves occasionally glimpsed into crystal balls, presciently foreseeing societal changes ahead. 'Metropolis' (1927), while not a war film, nevertheless envisioned a dystopian future of society split into two class extremes that seemed inevitable following the world wars.

All things considered, silent war films breathed life into still frames, drawing audiences into a concoction of raw human emotion, riveting storytelling and honest portrayals of societal sentiments. The lasting influence of these films, beyond their aesthetic and artistic contributions, is in their silent yet eloquent reflection of the societies from which they emerged.

The societal reflections found in silent films are not mere static mirrors of a bygone era. Instead, they form the cornerstones of a dynamic narrative, influencing war films' evolution, societal discourse, and our understanding of historical events. Thus, silent films do more than just entertain; they teach, enrage, provoke, and above all, reflect.

In conclusion, the Silent Era of war films tells the fascinating story of society's perceptions and attitudes towards war, love, and human resilience during the trials of warfare. Each film, in its unique way, documents and preserves the zeitgeist of the era, providing us a priceless window into our past and continuing to enrich our understanding of the intricate relationship between war, society, and cinema.

Pioneers and Iconic Silent War Films

As we delve deeper into the silent era of war films, it's high time we pay due tribute to the pioneers who shaped this genre, and explore some of the iconic silent war films that marked the early corpus of war cinema. The silent era was not silent by any means in its expression, rather, it allowed the makers to employ unique storytelling strategies unfettered by dialogue, relying on the intricate interplay of visuals, mise-en-scene, and title cards.

Distinctively, one of the earliest directors to distinguish himself in the arena of silent war films was D. W. Griffith. A master visual raconteur, Griffith's "The Birth of a Nation (1915)" remains a powerful, albeit controversial, epitome of silent war cinema. Despite its undeniable racially prejudiced narrative, the film's mammoth portrayal of the American Civil War with meticulously orchestrated battle sequences marked a turning point in cinema's representation of war.

Another film by Griffith, "Hearts of the World (1918)", further cemented his place as a pioneer. A war drama documenting the horrors of World War I, it used real battlefield footage mixed with fictional plot lines, merging reality with fiction and thereby setting a precedent in terms of subtlety and nuance in war cinema.

The advent of filmmakers like Abel Gance further pushed the boundaries of silent war films. Widely acknowledged as one of the most innovative directors of the era, Gance's monumental "J'accuse (1919)" is a distinct testimony to his genius. The film is a passionate anti-war narrative focusing on human loss, demonstrating the war's devastating impact on personal relationships, against the backdrop of World War I.

Hollywood's answer to the early silent war films pioneers was the multi-talented Charlie Chaplin, who seamlessly blended comic relief into the grimness of war. An example of the extent of his influence is the universally acclaimed "The Great Dictator (1940)". Although technically not a silent film, its roots in silent film techniques and its deliberate, dramatic use of sound make it a prominent touchstone from the transition period between silent and sound cinema.

Beyond Hollywood, the world witnessed several other pioneers who crafted striking silent war narratives. "The

Battleship Potemkin (1925)" by Sergei Eisenstein, for instance, still stands as a cinematic masterpiece. It dared to tell a revolutionary story shvesting power to the common people, capturing the essence of the 1905 Russian revolution.

An equally pivotal film, "Westfront 1918 (1930)" by G. W. Pabst hit the screens with a horrendous portrait of World War I. It remains a striking portrayal of the mix of heroic glamorization, socio-political conflicts, and, more strikingly, the glorified image of the enemy.

The silent era also gave us movies like "Wings (1927)" by William Wellman. A war/romance flick set against World War I, it presents a juxtaposition of the innocence of love with the brutality of war. It's no wonder it took home the first-ever Academy award for Best Picture.

Individually, each of these filmmakers and films leaves a remarkable legacy, and collectively, they laid the groundwork for war films as a distinctive genre. They took cinemagoers to the heart of battlefields, humanized soldiers, and infused a deeper understanding of wars' tragedies and triumphs.

On a wider societal radar, these films stirred emotions, provoked thoughts, and aligned public sentiments during war times. From igniting nationalism to criticizing war politics, they undoubtedly became a powerful tool shaping public opinion and collective memory of war.

Yet, an important angle to consider is the dialectical relationship between the pioneering filmmakers and the medium of film itself. These filmmakers were experimenting, yes, but their experimental attitude was fostered by the expanding capabilities of film. Silent cinema allowed a global language to take root, a visual vocabulary that transcended language barriers.

Indeed, the silent era of war films gave filmmakers a seemingly paradoxical power. On one hand, they had the ability to glorify war, to sanitize its realities, and to use it as a vehicle to propagate certain ideologies. On the other hand, they had the power to reveal war's grotesque underbelly, its tragic consequences on common people, its futility.

Our jaunt through the silent era shows that war films are never just about battles and their outcomes. They are a cultural artifact, a reflection of their time, a tool of influence, a testament to human frailties and, at their best, a beacon of human spirit and resilience. The pioneers of the silent era not only understood this, but they also had the audacity to experiment with these ideas, making a profound impact on war films and indeed on cinema itself.

As we transition from the silent era to the golden age of cinema, let's keep these lessons in mind. War is much more than conflict, and similarly, war movies are much more than mere depictions of war. They are fertile grounds of artistic, cultural, and political explorations, and it is this complex weave that we will untangle in the upcoming chapters.

Chapter 3: The Golden Age and WWII Cinema

The Golden Age of Hollywood hit its stride at a time of worldwide commotion, with WWII at the fore. This era, spanning from the late 1930s to the early 1950s, was a time when Hollywood set its sights on the global conflict. Arthurian spirit filled the air as WWII movies painted pictures of heroic warriors, each battling their own trials against the backdrop of a world in flames. They didn't merely depict the war; they became part of it, a catalyst that fueled the patriotic fervor of the masses. Interestingly, Hollywood mingled propaganda with artistry, blurring the lines between reality and film fantasy in a meaningful way. This era's cinema wasn't just about the fight on screen; it subtly stirred the emotions of the audience, nudging them towards a deep-seated patriotism. It was art, yes. But it was art with a mission.

But the end of the war didn't mark the end of its cinematic impact. In fact, the aftermath ripped open a new layer of social understanding, as society came to terms with the profound scars the war had left, not just on the soldiers, but on the world itself. Movies began to depict how societies struggled to return to normalcy post-war. From this bloomed a collection of poignant tales, stories that mirrored the harsh realities the war inflicted. This unmasked portrayal deeply influenced society, offering them a raw understanding of the consequences of warfare. The Golden Age was, in essence, Hollywood's brave plunge into enchanting narratives and daring storytelling, a masterful blend of art, propaganda, patriotism, and realism that continues to hold a golden spot in the annals of film history.

Hollywood's Take on World War II

The film industry's gripping depiction of World War II is radiant in its own unique way. Hollywood, a prominent voice in this respect, captured raw emotions, heroism and the raw impact of the war, creating a timeless genre which thrives even today. Movies set in this era transported audiences to the grueling front lines and home front, generating an emotional understanding of the global conflict.

The onset of World War II inspired Hollywood to create movies that featured the war itself – its impact, the reasons surrounding it, and the national sentiment towards it. Films like 'Casablanca', 'The Great Dictator', and 'To Be or Not To Be' became cultural signifiers that offered audiences a specific perspective on the war.

The manner in which Hollywood's perspective on World War II evolved is a topic worth exploring. Initially, films tended to be simple, portraying soldiers and national leaders as heroes fighting against villainous forces. As a result, these early war films, generally, were more about promoting nationalism and honoring the sacrifices made by the soldiers.

As the war progressed, so did the narratives. Films began portraying soldiers as regular individuals faced with harsh realities of life and death, anguish, and loss. This shift in perspective was witnessed in films like 'The Best years of Our Lives', and 'Since You Went Away' where war's stark reality and its impact on personal lives were evident. The narrative from the battle field shifted to the personal stories of soldiers and their families, underlining the profound human cost of war.

Allied with the government, Hollywood actively participated in making propaganda films to maintain national unity and morale during those distressful times. The purpose was multifaceted — to garner support for the ongoing war, to evoke patriotic feelings, and to make citizens conscious of the greater cause. 'Why We Fight', a documentary series commissioned by the U.S. government, offered a robust ideological justification for U.S. involvement in the war.

The cinematic representation of World War II wasn't always about the home front or the front line. Comedies such as 'The Major and the Minor' and 'Buck Privates', kept the audience's spirits high during turbulent times. Although these fell outside classical war narratives, they played their part in supporting the greater cause.

In stark contrast to these lighter films, towards the end of the war, Hollywood began producing films that questioned the very nature of the war and the impact it had on the people involved. One of such films is 'The Best Years Of Our Lives.' This film captured the struggles of war veterans as they readjusted to civilian life after facing the horrors of World War II.

In the following years, Hollywood's depiction of World War II began to shift from glorifying the conflict to criticizing it, showcasing the futility and trauma attached to it. The movies began mirroring the growing disenchantment of a war-torn society.

Notwithstanding the varying tones and themes of movies released, these films provided solace and escapism to a nation grappling with global discord. America's shared experiences were displayed on-screen, creating a collective narrative of World War II.

This period also saw groundbreaking technical advancements in filmmaking. New techniques were used to create realistic battle scenes, and creative innovations like film noir were introduced, leading to a rich and diverse cinematic era.

Hollywood's portrayals of World War II have left a lasting impact on cinema. The film industry provided not only historical perspective, but also a shared emotional narrative that influenced and shaped public opinion. These films bore the profound responsibility of uniting the nation and instilling hope during some of the darkest times in history.

The films from the World War II era offered audiences a glimpse into what war was like, its impact on both soldiers and civilians alike, and elucidated some of society's deepest fears, hopes, and dreams. The honest depictions led to a wave of social change and stirred discussions about war, peace, and humanity.

Hollywood has always been a reflection of societal sentiment and the films of World War II were no exception. This era of filmmaking was instrumental in shaping how the public perceived the war and played an enormous role in narrating the history of the times.

In summary, Hollywood's take on World War II was as multifaceted as the conflict itself. Whether offering introspective dramas, comedic relief, or morale-boosting propaganda films, the era left an indelible mark on cinema. The impact of this poignant era goes beyond its artistic contributions, reaching into the annals of social commentary and historical preservation.

Propaganda, Patriotism, and Art

As we delve further into the context and implications of war films during the Golden Age and World War II era, we must grasp the entangled concepts of propaganda, patriotism, and art in the realm of wartime cinema. These elements interweaved and transformed not only the cinematographic approach but also the societal understanding and attitude towards the war.

Cinema during World War II became a powerful tool of propaganda on both sides of the conflict. The United States War Department, recognizing the power of cinema, commissioned filmmakers to create movies with a clear agenda - stir up patriotic sentiments in the audience and depict enemy forces in negative light. The axis powers turned to the same tactic, harnessing the medium to galvanize their populations and fuel their war machines.

In America, Hollywood was enlisted in a mission. It was tasked to surge the public morale and promote the valor and heroism of American soldiers. Films like "Sergeant York" and "Mrs. Miniver" didn't shy away from underscoring the righteousness of the Allied cause while painting a grim picture of the Axis powers. They embodied a compelling fusion of patriotism and propaganda and succeeded in steering the public towards the support of their troops and their nation's endeavors in the war.

In presenting the heroic deeds of American soldiers, these films cultivated a profound sense of patriotism. Patriotic fervor wasn't just a byproduct of propaganda but an essential ingredient in these films. The audience, drawn to the cinema during these trying times, found comfort and hope in the narrative of their nation's gallantry, thus propagating cultural unity and strengthening the war effort at home.

But amidst the grand patriotic narrative and the presentation of war as a black and white affair, the artistry in these films remained just as potent. The narrative was carefully crafted, the characters were developed with depth, and cinematographic techniques were meticulously employed to produce films that were not just vehicles for propaganda, but also substantial works of art.

One might wonder if the informational aspect of these films impeded the creative vision of the artists behind them. On the contrary, many directors thrived in this climate of controlled storytelling. They carved narratives out of reality, laying a path for their viewers that led to a patriotic and positive conclusion. Every set, every dialogue, every soundtrack was a testament to their artistic prowess.

Emotion became the fulcrum of these films. It was weaved into the fabric of characters and plotlines, making the audience feel a personal connection with the abstract concept of war. This not only relayed the intended patriotic and propagandistic sentiments but also achieved a degree of profound and emotional artistry, anchored deeply in the human condition. The filmmakers were adroit at presenting the realities and consequences of war, albeit from a definitely consenting viewpoint, in a grander, emotionally textured narrative.

That's not to say that all war movies during this period were uncritical celebratory portrayals. There were films that subtly questioned the war or laid bare its devastating human cost. "Battleground" and "The Best Years of our Lives" captured the physical and psychological tolls of war on soldiers and their families, paving the way for more nuanced war narratives in future decades.

After all, films are both a mirror and a mold of society. They reflect the milieu of their creation, and in doing so, they have the power to shape cultural sentiments. While World War II era films were tools of propaganda and patriotism, they teetered on a delicate balance of being an artistic medium and a political instrument.

As the war ended, and with the dawning of a new world order, war films began altering their approach. The black and white narrative slowly greyed as films began exploring the complexities of war. Yet, the influence of World War II war movies lingered, leaving an indelible mark on the collective cultural memory and shaping the course of cinematic narratives to come.

In summary, World War II era saw a distinctive intertwining of propaganda, patriotism, and art to serve a larger purpose - the war effort. It was a demonstration of how cinema, in a time of conflict and patriotism, can rise beyond entertainment into an influential cultural tool, transforming the social fabric while etching powerful narratives and images in the national psyche.

The curious interplay of propaganda, patriotism and art has left a lasting impression on the world of cinema. It altered our perception of war, heroes and villains, and history itself. This era also offers us a chilling yet fascinating glance into the power of cinema as a tool for manipulation, unification and emotional resonance. It's more than a mere retrospective look at bygone times; it's an exploration of the complex relationship between art, its creators and its audience amid the turmoil and crisis of a world at war.

Looking forward, that confluence of propaganda, patriotism, and art stands as a testament to the power of cinema in molding societal perspective and the role war films can play in shaping our understanding of conflicts, past, present, and yet to come.

Impact on Post-War Society

The impact of World War II on cinema wasn't simply limited to the appearance of war-themed movies; it went beyond the realms of the cinematic world and seeped into the society in the post-war era. Indeed, the depiction of war on the cinematic canvas left an indelible imprint on individuals and society as a whole.

Following the conclusion of the war, there was an explosion of films depicting the horrors and heroism of the worldwide conflict. Such films played a significant role in shaping public perception of the war. They served as a cultural mirror, reflecting society's beliefs and attitudes at the time. The war films reached a large audience, influencing the collective memory of the war and directly affecting public opinion about the war and its aftermath.

Moreover, the Golden Era war films also had an educational impact. Many people lacked firsthand knowledge of the war, either because they hadn't experienced it directly or because they were born after it ended. War films provided these viewers with a vicarious experience and knowledge about the war. They became a primary source of education and information for many about the political, cultural, and human factors that shaped the world's most cataclysmic event.

These films also contributed to a sense of national identity. War movies often portrayed the country's soldiers as heroes fighting the good fight against evil forces. This portrayal fostered a sense of pride and unity among the viewers, creating a narrative of nationalistic righteousness.

The post-war era was also a time of great upheaval, with society struggling to come to terms with the consequences of the war. The economic, social, and psychological scars caused by the war were depicted and explored in films. These portrayals added to the public discourse about these issues, creating a space for dialogue and reflection.

In addition, war films played a notable role in shaping gender roles in society. During the war, women had, out of necessity, taken up roles traditionally held by men. Contrarily, the films of the era often clung firmly to traditional gender roles. Consequently, this perpetuated societal norms, influencing the push for women to return to domestic roles.

The portrayal of war also gave a voice to marginalized groups. Specifically, they highlighted the roles played by African American soldiers who, despite the segregation policies of the time, served their country. Providing a platform for these stories in mainstream cinema was a stepping stone toward equality.

The power of storytelling in film also highlighted the devastation of war, influencing a movement for peace. Having recently experienced the most destructive conflict in human history, society was more conscious of the adverse effects of war, inspiring a drive toward maintaining peace. War films served to remind viewers of the consequences of war, reinforcing this desire for peace.

The films of this period dealt with post-traumatic stress and its impact on soldiers returning home from war. For the first time, cinema began to address this disorder explicitly, calling attention to the plight of veterans and encouraging society to provide them with the support and help they needed.

In terms of technology, the Golden Age of cinema saw the development of new filming techniques. The innovations made during the war, such as handheld cameras, were incorporated into cinematic production, transforming the way films were made and influencing the movies of later generations.

There was also a rise in anti-war sentiment reflected in movies. While early depictions glorified war and soldiers, the realities of war and its devastating effects led to a shift in narrative. A number of films began to question the motives and fallout of war, pushing society toward introspection.

Reflecting on the societal impact of war films in the post-World War II era, it becomes clear how intertwined cinema and society are. These films served multiple roles, educating the public, shaping their opinions, challenging societal norms, and even influencing political discourse.

Meanwhile, they also influenced entertainment and style trends. The movies of the era had a major impact on fashion, music, and lifestyle, shaping pop culture and even influencing architecture and design trends into the '50s and '60s.

In ending, as filmmakers unpacked the war, they were not only reflecting a snapshot of their time, but also weaving a narrative tapestry that would inform future generations of the soldiers' courage and sacrifice, the devastation wrought by war, and the resilience of the human spirit.

The impact of war movies on the post-war society, therefore, extends beyond the realm of mere entertainment. It becomes a means of understanding and reflecting on our history, shaping our identity, and addressing our future ñ proof that film has the potential for more than just storytelling, but for change.

Chapter 4: The Cold War on Screen

As we traverse the timeline of war films, it's impossible to overlook the shadowy complexity of the Cold War years. Film had become a canvas for humanity's anxieties, encapsulating the unspoken tensions that plagued society during the Cold War era. The dramatic dichotomy between capitalism and communism, and the silent but potent chess match between superpowers, inspired an epoch of creativity that birthed a new genre of war films. These weren't just blood and battle anymore. They mirrored the invisible fight — a covert war of influence fueling paranoia and suspicion. Here, filmmakers had to negotiate the thin line between cultural anxiety and censorship, resulting in a cinematic landscape marked by great innovation and symbolic storytelling. This era was illustrative of how cinema could be a reflection of the zeitgeist but also a tool for framing public perception. The films from this period not only captured the essence of a divided world but also paved the way for novel interpretative approaches to war and conflict. So, we plunge into the gripping narrative of the Cold War on screen, embracing its layered dimensions and recognizing its contribution to the course of war cinema.

Filming the Invisible Battle

As we delve into the representation of the Cold War on film, one thing becomes palpably clear – the challenge lay in capturing an invisible battle. The Cold War was far less about the battlefield's physical realities, as was integral to World

War II, and more about the psychological, ideological, and political battle of the ages. This invisible battle, between capitalism and communism, fear and reality, often left no tangible destruction, but deeply scarred the collective psyche of nations involved and reverberated through cinema.

The art of filming the invisible battle meant engaging the audience in this silence of real war action. The depiction had to revolve around the covert operations, the political tension, and the persistent sense of fear, providing a stark contrast to other war films where the action was paramount. Atomic paranoia, espionage, and covert operations became the new battlefield, as showcased in films like "Dr. Strangelove" or "Fail Safe". These movies often took place in boardrooms, control rooms, or aircrafts instead of trenches or war fronts.

During this era, we witness a shift in narrative technique. Character growth takes precedence over plot, the emotional turmoil within the characters showing the psychological impact of the invisible battle. For example, the characters in "The Manchurian Candidate" are planted firmly in this emotional struggle, revealing the fear and paranoia prevalent during the era. Traditionally villainous characters are no longer individual soldiers or generals, but far-reaching, faceless entities representing different forms of government.

Settings, too, played a crucial role in depicting this invisible battle. Rather than portraying unscathed cities as mere backgrounds, cities themselves became integral parts of the story. Washington D.C, Manhattan, Moscow- they became silent witnesses to the psychological cold war, assisting audiences in contextualizing the narrative of the invisible battle into their reality. Films like "Seven Days in May" and "The Day the Earth Stood Still" exemplify this shift in setting roles.

Broadly speaking, visual imagery took on a more symbolic role in films. For instance, the mushroom cloud became an iconic image of the era, showcasing the omnipresent nuclear threat. It stood as a visual shorthand, engaging the audience with its ominous, terrifying implications while needing no explicit description. This use of symbolic visual theatrics helped encapsulate the invisible battle's essence.

The era was not without its experiments either. Directors took risks, challenging traditional filmmaking norms. Non-linear narratives gained momentum, allowing filmmakers to delve deeper into psychological intricacies. Movies such as "La Jetée" were revolutionary, presenting a narrative based on still pictures to encapsulate the philosophical musings of time, memory, and post-apocalyptic existence. This film, as well as others like it, depicted the internal, invisible battle within humans, rather than external conflicts.

Allied with these experimental narratives, the changing landscape of cinematography also aided in filming these invisible battles. Directors began utilizing experimental editing techniques, match cuts, and unique camera angles to navigate the story's intricacies and complexities. Stanley Kubrick's "2001: A Space Odyssey", amongst others, exemplifies these subtle shifts in filming techniques that beautifully captured the invisible war.

The use of sound is another significant shift in this era. Distinct techniques developed to represent the 'invisible,' be it through haunting silence, abrupt sound shifts, or jarring crescendos. The shift from diegetic to non-diegetic sound added layers to the narrative, creating a sense of unease and tension in many Cold War films. The unsettling musical score in "The Birds" perfectly encapsulates this concept.

While the mainstream classical Hollywood style of filmmaking persisted, pockets of rebellion against the system arose. The French New Wave and Italian Neorealism presented radical changes in filmmaking techniques that heavily impacted the filming of the invisible battle. These movements rejected traditional storytelling, explored personal narratives, and embraced unconventional filmmaking methods, providing an alternate vision for presenting the Cold War's narrative.

Additionally, the rise of television also impacted how the invisible battles were filmed. Television series like "The Twilight Zone" explored Cold War anxieties through speculative fiction, often portraying dystopian futures. This approach allowed filmmakers to incorporate metaphoric references to the Cold War, thereby adding an additional layer to their storytelling.

On the one hand, Hollywood produced spy thrillers like "Tinker Tailor Soldier Spy", using suspense, mystery, and intelligent plotting to mirror Cold War tensions. On the other hand, there were satirical films like "The Russians Are Coming, the Russians Are Coming" serving as social commentaries on the era's absurd paranoia.

In essence, the invisible battle of the Cold War era brought about a paradigm shift in war films. The physical carnage of World War II had given way to the intangible, cerebral battles that stemmed from paranoia and fear. The evolution of this cinematic phenomenon paved the way for more profound narrative complexity, character depth, and experimentation in storytelling techniques. It challenged filmmakers to weave narratives around subtle and unseen battles, a valuable filmmaking skill that transcends eras and remains relevant in contemporary cinema.

As we move forward, let us delve deeper into this unconscious societal anxiety and how its cinematic representation has evolved over time.

Cultural Anxiety and Cinema

Cinema has always been a mirror that reflects society's complexities. When the world was in the throes of the Cold War, filmmakers too were wrestling with their anxieties and fears. The fear of nuclear annihilation, the constant suspicions, and the ideological divides seeped into the cinematic world, giving birth to a unique wave of films that were rich in tension and paranoia. Directors and screenwriters became conduits, channeling this cultural anxiety into the heart of their narratives, shaping an era of filmmaking that still deeply resonates with audiences today.

Every great film starts with a potent seed of inspiration. With the looming threat of nuclear war and ideological differences sparking suspicions, there was no shortage of material for filmmakers to draw upon in this era. They wove narratives that revolved around secret agents, brinkmanship, spies, and saboteurs, all the while maintaining an undercurrent of tension. The stakes were high, the anxiety palpable, and the narratives riveting with suspense.

Creeping into the human consciousness was a growing sense of fear and dread. The nuclear arms race and the proliferation of espionage pushed people to the edge of their seats. It was a fear that was both esoteric and explicit. It couldn't be escaped, and unavoidably, it found its way into the films of the time. Movie theatres became arenas where cultural anxiety was confronted head-on, often with a stark, brutal honesty.

The cinematic landscape of this era was laden with films that reflected the palpable fear of the Cold War period. Anti-communism sentiments were rampant, and themes of espionage ran rampant. It was a world inhabited by characters who were ever vigilant, facing invisible enemies and cloaked threats. Such narratives successfully echoed the silent dread then consuming society, bringing the real life tension to the silver screen.

Cinema also became an instrument through which filmmakers could subtly challenge and question prevailing ideologies. The paranoia induced by the Red Scare granted filmmakers the license to explore more mysterious and suspenseful plotlines. However, beneath the surface level entertainment existed insightful commentary about the broader societal and political dynamics at play.

Undoubtedly, the thematic essence of these films was culturally sensitive. To successfully tread this complex terrain, filmmakers had to strike a balance between emotional maturity and political delicacy. They sought to tell stories that were both politically engaging and emotionally resonant, requiring them to navigate the delicate dance between controversy and sensitivity.

Constant peril and invisible foes gave room to a new breed of movie heroes. The archetype of the secret agent, epitomized by characters like James Bond, came to the limelight. These characters were sleek, suave, and dangerously intelligent, appealing to audiences with their audacity and courage in the face of insurmountable odds.

However, heroes were not the only focal point for this breed of film. The societal fear of a nuclear Armageddon also led filmmakers to explore catastrophic scenarios. Filmmakers dared to ask, "What if the unthinkable happened?" Thus, the atomic monster genre emerged, featuring colossal creatures brought to life by nuclear radiation. These films weren't just a spectacle; they were a satirical take on humanity's insistence on tampering with destructive technology.

The depiction of nuclear anxiety and Cold War tensions also reflected societal insecurities and mistrust. Films began to experiment with narrative form and structure, echoing the fractured and divided nature of global politics at the time.

In such a volatile atmosphere, cinema played multiple roles —it was a catharsis, a platform for dialogue, and a safe refuge. It allowed society to engage with fear, to face dread head-on in a controlled space. Thus, anxiety found a release and fears a refuge on the silver screen.

In conclusion, the cultural anxiety of the Cold War era left an indelible mark on the cinema of the time. Filmmakers tread the delicate line of reflecting societal fears while providing a subliminal commentary about larger sociopolitical dynamics. Through their narratives, they held up a mirror to society's deepest fears and apprehensions, helping audiences confront and better understand the cultural anxieties of their time. Thus, films became a crucial part of the broader social and political discourse, helping shape and reflect the anxieties of an era.

Cinema during the Cold War was not just about entertainment; it became an exploration of dating a nuclear annihilation and rampant ideological political tensions. As the lines between real life and film blurred, the power of cinema to reflect cultural anxiety and to provoke thought increased exponentially. Films became more than an escape from reality; they were a plunge into the very heart of fear and tension that characterized society.

Thus, the section explores how cinema serves as an echo chamber for societal anxieties, reflecting them in its narratives, characters, and themes. With the Cold War serving as an eerie backdrop, cinema morphed into a mirror of cultural apprehensions, exploring and pushing the boundaries of societal fears while at the same time providing a platform for confrontation, dialogue, and catharsis.

Whether represented through spy thrillers or nuclear catastrophe films, cultural anxiety found a voice in cinema, illustrating just how intrinsically linked the art form is with the social and political climate of its period. This era of filmmaking, characterized by its embodiment of Cold War anxiety and cultural tensions, continues to engage, horrify, and enthrall audiences, reaffirming the cinema's enduring power to capture the essence of the human condition.

Cinematic Innovation in a Divided Era

The Cold War, a period of global tension primarily between the United States and the Soviet Union, held the world on the edge. It was a divisive time, and cinema, as a mirror to society, reflected this divide. The metamorphosis of the art form during this icy divide carried significant innovations, incorporating elements beyond the screen to make emotional connections with the audience.

For instance, film soundtracks started playing a more interactive role, weaving a deeper connection between the narrative and audience. As we see in films like 'Doctor Zhivago' or 'The Manchurian Candidate,' the soundtrack became an essential tool for setting a film's tone. Symphonic music, experimental drone effects, and traditional folk songs all added texture to the cinematic experience.

Another remarkable innovation in this era was the use of color. Color was creatively manipulated to subliminally communicate various moods or emotions. Color schemes became deeply tied to a Film's narrative, often carrying symbolic or metaphorical connotations.

Artistic ingenuity also extended to film marketing during this period. Beyond just selling movie tickets, marketing campaigns began to leverage pop culture, current events, and societal anxieties to stir public interest. It was during this time that the concept of blockbuster releases and tie-in products took root, initiating a new way of making and promoting movies.

In addition, the Cold War era saw an interesting cross-pollination of genres within war films. Spy thrillers, psychological dramas, and documentaries all lent elements to the war film genre, making it multifaceted and dynamic.

Films like 'The Bedford Incident' mixed elements of suspense thrillers with war film tropes to drive home the paranoia felt during the Cold War. On the other hand, 'Paths of Glory' leaned into the drama genre, providing a deeper and more human exploration of war. This blend of genres provided audiences with refreshing perspectives on war, widening the genre's appeal.

Moreover, non-linear storytelling began to take root in war films during the Cold War era. As embodied in films like 'The Manchurian Candidate,' narratives began to weave intricate labyrinths of flashbacks, flash-forwards, and dream sequences. These complex storytelling techniques allowed filmmakers to explore war's psychological dimensions with greater depth.

The Cold War also saw Hollywood experimenting with global film productions. This was a strategic move, aimed at countering the Soviet Union's film influence across Europe and Asia. Filmmaker collaborations transcended national borders, creating a mosaic of different cultural perspectives within a single piece of cinema.

Besides, a significant rise in the popularity of film festivals also had a strong impact on war films' stylistic evolution during the Cold War era. Prestigious festivals like the Cannes Film Festival or the Berlinale provided filmmakers with an international platform to showcase their art. This undoubtedly encouraged a surge of innovative, artistic, and non-conformist war films during this period.

This era also saw the birth of a new type of film - the disaster film. Movies like 'Dr. Strangelove' utilized a mixture of satire and terror to illustrate the absolute horror of nuclear war. These films provided an alternative to traditional war movies, presenting war's realistic horrors through fictional scenarios.

A noticeable trend during this era was the incorporation of hard-hitting dialogue and ideological exchange rather than physical conflict. This narrative approach mirrored the indirect confrontations that characterized the Cold War. The dialogue wasn't just a conveyor of plot, but a complex weaver of ideologies and philosophies.

Adding to this, the method acting technique gained prominence during the Cold War period. This approach required actors to fully immerse themselves in their character's thoughts and feelings, producing performances of raw emotional intensity that powerfully communicated the human cost of war.

Looking back, it's clear that the war film genre underwent significant transformation during the Cold War era. The artistic and technological innovations birthed during this period not only augmented the war film genre, but also left an indelible mark on the broader landscape of cinema. This tremendous era of innovation embodied the paradox of the Cold War - dividing society and art forms while simultaneously reviving and reinventing them.

As we look forward to the next section, we will explore how the cinema industry took another radical turn in its portrayal of warfare during the Vietnam era. Join us as we delve further into the transformation of war films, through the lens of realism, raw emotion, and the influence of societal movements.

Chapter 5: Vietnam War- A Cinematic Revolution

As we delve deeper into the annals of war cinema, we encounter the cinematic revolution sparked by the Vietnam War, an era marked by raw emotive exposure and cutting realism. This new era of storytelling superseded the theatrical heroics of yesteryears, instead showcasing the grim facets of warfare with riveting precision. It was a time when filmmakers swore allegiance to the compelling truth, unmasking the fallacies of past glorification and belying chivalric tales with more authentic narratives. Enmeshed in this fierce battlefield of credibility were influential directors whose daring visions refused to be curtailed, their very creations not merely vestiges of cinematic craft, but potent embodiments of societal critique. In portraying the vehement protest movement that surged in America, they masterfully merged wakeful audacity with undeniable artistry, reclaiming cinema as a powerful instrument of societal introspection. It was during this tumultuous epoch that films like "Apocalypse Now" and "Full Metal Jacket" seared into public consciousness, addressing the heart-wrenching predicaments of wartime with breathtaking clarity. The impact of these films both on contemporaneous audiences and future war cinemas would prove to be indelible and irrevocable, reshaping the manner in which warfare was perceived, represented, and critiqued. This insightful exploration into societal realities also provoked a long overdue discourse on the physical and psychological toll war exacts on soldiers, revealing the untold aftermath of combat. In short, the cinematic revolution sparked by the Vietnam War underscored the power of celluloid realism, altering the trajectory of war films forever.

Realism and Raw Emotion

The Vietnam War heralded not only a substantial shift in the geopolitical landscape but also significantly reshaped the cinematic treatment of warfare. Films began to veer from the previously established templates of glory and valor, integrating elements of realism and raw emotion that unraveled the perceived nobility of battle. To truly comprehend the seismic shift, consider the 1978 film "The Deer Hunter", directed by Michael Cimino. This film exposed audiences to the brutal realities of war and the lasting impact it has on soldiers and society.

"The Deer Hunter" disregards the simplistic portrayal of soldiers and presents the gut-wrenching loss, despair, and disillusionment they experienced. This film's depiction of the harrowing game of Russian roulette, played by POWs, was undeniably gut-wrenching. Although not confirmed as a historical occurrence, this disturbing portrayal serves as an uncomfortable metaphor for the senseless loss and the hazardous unpredictability of warfare.

The emphasis on the soldier's psychological and emotional journey also adds an unvarnished sense of realism that illustrates the toll of combat on their human spirit. This elevation of human experiences in the context of war starkly contrasts the idealized war heroes of earlier films.

Another film that profoundly impacted audiences is Oliver Stone's "Platoon," released in 1986. This film hones in on the veritable chaos that engulfs a platoon of American soldiers in Vietnam. Stone's personal experiences as an infantryman in Vietnam serve as the core of the film's narrative, intern lending the film a tangible authenticity and personal resonance.

Throughout "Platoon," the audience sees the protagonist Chris Taylor, an educated and innocent young man, grapple with combat realities, the abhorrent acts committed by those in his platoon, and the untenable moral dilemmas he faces. The story arc traces a clear transformation of his character, signifying the deep-seated effects of war trauma and the corrosion of moral values.

The graphic depiction of ruthless violence and moral degradation in "Platoon" starkly illustrated the darker aspects of the American military presence in Vietnam. This strain of brutal realism was a notable departure from the more restrained, often heroic, depictions of war seen in previous eras of cinema.

Coppola's "Apocalypse Now" also stands as a pillar of this shift. It's a surreal blend of horror, madness, and the quest for cause, paralleling Joseph Conrad's "Heart of Darkness." It visualizes the descent into a state of utter insanity and lawlessness, where the perception of right and wrong blurs and even dissipates.

In "Apocalypse Now," the U.S. Army Captain Willard's journey to assassinate Colonel Kurtz, a rogue army officer, illuminates an apocalypse inward, a slide into personal chaos paralleling the mayhem of war. The film delves deep into the psyche of its characters, leading to an exploration of profound existential questions concerning morality, sanity, and the human condition.

Quite contrary to 'bombastic' war epics, "Apocalypse Now" weaves a hallucinatory narrative, unveiling warfare as a horrific theater of the absurd. It veers from the clear dichotomy of good and evil, honor and deceit, instead pushing viewers into a moral labyrinth that precisely mirrors the senseless intricacy of war.

Realism is fundamental to understanding war, but so too is the raw emotion that war evokes. A noteworthy mention here is "Full Metal Jacket," a film by Stanley Kubrick, filled with metaphors that strip away the commonplace notions about war. The raw emotion and themes discussed in the film communicate an antithetical perspective of valor and heroism in warfare.

"Full Metal Jacket" divides itself into two halves, one at the Marine Corps boot camp where the dehumanization and transformation of individuals into battle-ready Marines occur, and the second in Vietnam, where the gruesome realities of war set in. This duality presents an uncensored view of the war, unshrouded by the glorifying narratives for historical events, thus emphasizing the brutal actualities of this dreadful experience.

These films broke ground, rejecting romantic idealizations of war, and in their stead, harboring an uncompromising commitment to represent the war in its most destructive, dehumanizing form. They demanded audiences to acknowledge the hidden faces of war, the faces distorted by pain, marked by fear, and stripped of their identities.

The introduction of realism and the raw emotion in the cinematic portrayal of the Vietnam war era significantly shaped the collective consciousness about war's realities. These films are not just a record of history; they are primary lenses through which future generations will perceive, understand, and form opinions about past wars.

Overall, war films pivoted towards complex narratives that offer no moral certitudes but pose timely, often discomforting, questions about humanity's darker aspects. It's a cinema that refuses to look away, fomenting discussions on violence, integrity, and the true cost of war that reverberate long beyond the end credits roll.

The Protest Movement and Film

The Vietnam War stands as one of the most controversial conflicts in modern history, sparking widespread protest and dissent. Not only was it a battle fought in the jungles of Vietnam, but it sparked a war for the mind and the heart of the American populace - a battle often fought on the celluloid screen.

This era of turbulence and protest seeped into the cinematic crevices, marking a revolutionary change in the way war was represented on film. The heavy hand of propaganda and romance that characterized earlier depictions of war gave way to a raw, gritty realism. The polished heroes of yesteryear were replaced with flawed men, grappling with the moral implications of their actions.

As the youth of America began to question the value of war and challenge establishment norms, filmmakers reflected this rebellion in their craft. The cinema of the Vietnam era arguably became a tool of the protest movement, painting a portrait of a war ridden with ambiguity and disillusionment.

Critical films challenged the notion of war as a straightforward battle of good versus evil. Instead, they portrayed a more complex interplay of moral shades of gray. They dared to ask difficult questions about the nature of valor, the meaning of patriotism, and the cost of unquestioning obedience.

A striking characteristic of Vietnam War films is the ambiguity they present. The enemy isn't always clearly defined; the line between the virtuous and the villainous often blurred. The harrowing realities of war, such as civilian casualties and the severe psychological toll on soldiers, were laid bare.

The cinema of this era reflected the atmosphere of dissent, suspicion, and anti-establishment sentiment that permeated American society. War films evolved from mere entertainment or propaganda tools into a vehicle for dialogue and introspection about war, politics, and societal norms.

These films challenged viewers' complacency and comfort, offering a visceral portrayal of the horrors of war. No longer could audiences remain detached from the travesties happening halfway around the world; they were served uncomfortably raw and close to home.

Films like "Platoon" and "Apocalypse Now" painted dismal portraits of war, steeped in moral ambiguity. They sought to cut through the inherent patriotism associated with war and peered into the bleak reality faced by soldiers. The Vietnam War, through the lenses of these visionary filmmakers, was a descent into madness than a heroic endeavor.

As the lines between combatants and civilians faded, so did the boundary between war front and home front. The ambiguities and ethical questions that arose from these films echoed the sentiments of a public growing increasingly disillusioned with military action and the government's narrative.

Simultaneously, these films served as a platform to represent unique perspectives often sidelined in traditional war narratives. Feminist and anti-racist movements, gaining traction during this era, found expression in war films that incorporated narratives of women and African Americans - groups that, too, bore the brunt of the war.

This period of intense social and political change challenged filmmakers to think critically and radically about the stories they told and the motifs they employed. The dominos effect created by the protest movement and the social unrest of the time propelled significant shifts in war filmmaking, changes that continue to reverberate in contemporary war cinema.

Indeed, the relevance of the Vietnam War era to film history lies not so much in the number of Academy Awards its films clinched, but in how it reshaped the narrative of war on screen. It redefined the battleground not as a heroic battlefield, but a murky plane of moral quandary that reflected the complexities of the world off-screen.

By exploring the uncomfortable truths of war and unraveling the intricacies of politics and human nature, these films not only reflected the socio-political landscape of their time but also spurred critical thought and conversation among their audiences. In doing so, they underscored the role of cinema as not only a mirror to society but an active participant in molding public discourse.

The protest movement redirected cinema's lens to the less-romanticized aspects of war, revealing a narrative unafraid to scrutinize patriotism, question militarization, and seek truth amidst chaos. The imprint of this era on war films persists, reminding us that art and war are inexorably linked in their ability to shape collective memory, identity, and perception.

Notable Directors and Films

The transition from the silent era and the Golden Age to the films of the Cold War and Vietnam War era was smooth, yet impactful. The causes and complexities of war were deepseated in the fabric of these films and several noteworthy directors took it upon themselves to challenge and alter the perception of war, paving the way for innovative cinematic storytelling.

Stanley Kubrick, a master of cinema, directed the iconic war film 'Paths of Glory' which is celebrated as a seminal piece of anti-war cinema. Kubrick's narrative technique focusing on the futile rituals of war commendably brought to life the dehumanizing cost of conflict.

'Dr. Strangelove or: How I Learned to Stop Worrying and Love the Bomb', also directed by Kubrick, is another iconic film. Its depiction of Cold War sensibilities, apocalyptic fear and satire communicated an ironic view of warfare making it a definitive masterpiece in war cinema.

In contrast, Francis Ford Coppola's 'Apocalypse Now' presented a harrowing vision of war. With its dark and intense narrative, it took upon the task of dissecting the moral confusion and madness of the Vietnam War. This surreal exploration of war proved that cinema can indeed be a crude reflection of geopolitical conflicts.

Coppola's contemporary, Oliver Stone, who himself was a Vietnam War veteran, made the Oscar-winning 'Platoon'. This film is unique in its autobiographical approach that critiques the U.S. military engagement in Vietnam.

Similarly, Michael Cimino's 'The Deer Hunter' offers a devastating look at the physical and psychological effects of the Vietnam War on American soldiers. Its intense storytelling and character exploration has made it one of the most recognizable war films.

On the other hand, Sidney Lumet's 'Fail-Safe', presented a grim and realistic portrayal of nuclear warfare, capturing the tension of the Cold War period with its intense drama and strong performances.

Stanley Kramer's 'On the Beach', is another compelling narrative revolving around the threat of nuclear devastation that encapsulated the paranoia of the post-World War era.

'M*A*S*H', directed by Robert Altman, took a different approach by combining comedy with war, making it a pioneering film that used humor to reflect on the absurdities of war.

Coming to more contemporary times, Steven Spielberg's 'Saving Private Ryan' is a glaring example of potent storytelling that realistically represented the horrors of World War II, taking war cinema to an unprecedented level of authenticity.

Ridley Scott's 'Black Hawk Down', highlighted the US military's troubled intervention in Somalia in 1993. Its gritty visualization and authentic depiction of modern warfare were highly impactful.

'The Hurt Locker', directed by Kathryn Bigelow, is a modern classic that looked at the Iraq War through the lens of a bomb disposal squad, engaging the audience with an intense and jittery narrative.

Another significant film, 'Charlie Wilson's War', directed by Mike Nichols, explored the geopolitics of the Soviet-Afghan War. This film, with its dramatization of real events, offered a critical look at American foreign policy and military intervention.

Collectively, these directors and their films have been instrumental in shaping the genre of war cinema. In exploring different facets of war, they have offered different perspectives on militaristic ideologies, politics of war, and personal experiences of conflict.

Ultimately, what makes these directors and films noteworthy is their ability to enhance our understanding of war by using cinema as a medium of reflection and critique. Their courage in questioning the convention, presenting diverse viewpoints, and pushing the boundaries of storytelling, have forever changed the landscape of war cinema.

Even as we move forward into exploring modern warfare in films, the contribution of these directors and their films serves as a continual reminder of the power of cinema and its ability to affect and inform our perception of war and conflict.

Chapter 6: Modern Warfare in Film

As we step into the realm of modern warfare on film, it's undeniable that technology has forcefully taken the helm, giving filmmakers newer, more realistic tools to work with. Such advancements have considerably reshaped the representation of warfare, gracing the silver screen with shockingly omnipresent, palpable experiences. Socio-political panoramas have shifted too, coloring our perceptions of modern conflicts differently. Ingenious cinematic explorations in movies like "Black Hawk Down", "The Hurt Locker", and "American Sniper" deliver stark, bracing perspectives on the wars in Somalia, Iraq, and Afghanistan. Additionally, specific genres have emerged, with thrillers focusing on counter-terrorism and drone warfare absorbing audiences into a nerve-wracking, yet fascinating, world of global defense strategy and moral ambiguities. Throughout this technological and thematic evolution, cinema's engagement with modern warfare perpetually tests the boundaries between fiction and reality, shaping and reflecting a world in a state of constant flux.

Technological Advancements

Within the realm of cinema, advances in technology have continuously shaped the trajectory of war films. It's necessary to delve into these advancements to interpret how war films have taken dramatic steps forward, integrating viewers more into the narrative than ever before.

In the early years, war films relied heavily on practical effects and miniatures to portray large-scale combat. Resourceful directors and production designers used a combination of miniature models, forced perspective, and clever camera tricks to deliver an illusion of grandeur and scope. However, these methods were often restrictive and could only yield convincing results to a certain extent.

Moving out of the Silent Era, synchronized sound technology arose in the late 1920s, sparking a seismic shift in filmmaking. The introduction of sound in war films not only amplified the realism but also the emotional intensity. The screams of soldiers, the explosive sounds of gunfire, the eerie whistles of falling bombs - these elements immersed the audiences' senses, painting a more vivid picture of the trials of warfare.

Shortly thereafter, the advent of color film marked another significant transition in the landscape of war films. The transition from black-and-white to color brought plenty to the table — one could argue that nothing harrowingly encapsulates the stark realities of war more than the deep crimson of spilled blood on a soldier's uniform, or the way flames dance violently against the inky black backdrop of the night. Indeed, color film seemed to breathe life, however brutal, into war stories.

Then came the 1970s, which brought about innovative camera techniques and movement. For example, handheld camera technology allowed war films to adopt a more documentary-style approach, placing viewers directly into the heart of battle. This was further revolutionized with the introduction of Steadicam technology, which provided smooth, dynamic, and immersive cinematographic sequences while preserving the organic feel of handheld footage.

Advancements in sound design also significantly influenced the portrayal of war. Dolby Surround sound systems and later iterations not only enhanced spatial awareness of sound but also emulated the chaos and kineticism of war, making the viewers feel like they were in the center of the war zone.

In the 1990s, the application of computer-generated imagery (CGI) began its dominance in the film industry. With CGI, the limit was truly the sky, and directors could now portray epic-scale battles and extravagant destruction that was otherwise impossible or impractical to achieve with physical sets, miniatures, or practical effects.

However, the utilization of CGI in war films was, and continues to be, a loaded factor. While it paved the way for seamless and stunning visual effects, it could also lead to unrealistic portrayals if not used judiciously. CGI, without doubt, can make the impossible possible, but it can equally risk undermining the brutal realism that a war film should ideally portray.

Fast-forward to the modern era, cutting-edge technology has enormously influenced war films' narratives. For instance, the development of drone technology allowed for expansive aerial views of warzones, offering a birds' eye perspective that was both awe-inspiring and somber.

Additionally, the recent advent of virtual reality (VR) and augmented reality (AR) indicated a promising possibility for war film narratives. A greater sense of immersion could be achieved by allowing spectators to literally step into the shoes of soldiers, or witness a battlefield unfold around them in 360 degrees. This could revolutionize the way audiences understand and experience the traumas, triumphs, and tragedies of warfare.

Apart from the on-screen transformations, technological advancements have also had a significant impact behind the scene. Modern editing software immensely expedited the filmmaking process, making it easier to manipulate shots, sound, and even performances to weave a more nuanced narrative.

Moreover, digital cinema cameras and high-definition filming meant that films could be shot with impressive clarity, contributing immensely to crafting visually stunning war films. On top of this, advanced sound recording and mixing technology have enabled the creation of a hyperrealistic aural experience, adding another layer to the immersive visual experience.

As we journey down this winding road, it's crucial to remember that the heart of war films isn't merely elevated by technology but intensely human narratives that define them. The visceral experience is undeniably accentuated by the application of technology, but it's the emotion, the sacrifice, the horrific beauty, the heroism, the despair, the camaraderie that truly grips the audience and leaves an indelible mark.

Thus, while technology enables us to expand the bounds of cinematic storytelling, great war films are not merely visual or auditory spectacles. They serve as visceral reminders of our shared humanity: our capacity for courage, compassion, and hope in the face of profound adversity and horror.

Society's View on Modern Conflicts

The advent of modern warfare on the big screen reshaped and simultaneously mirrored society's perception of war in profound ways. As symbols of society's values and cultural norms, films offer a unique lens through which we can dissect and discuss society's understanding and apprehension of contemporary conflicts.

Fundamentally, the modern conflict narrative in cinema is often punctuated by moral ambiguity, reflecting a departure from the clear-cut good versus evil dichotomy prevalent in earlier war films. The protagonist is no longer exclusively the chivalrous hero defending an irrefutable cause. Instead, we see characters wrestle with moral conflicts, sometimes blurring the line between hero and anti-hero, reflecting society's increasing skepticism towards the inherent righteousness of war.

This newfound ambiguity within war films is not merely a cinematic curiosity, but a reflection of contemporary society's sentiments. Today's audience is more informed and aware, accustomed to questioning authority and the justifications offered for war. We are living in an era of unprecedented access to information and differing perspectives, reflecting a skepticism that war films have duly acknowledged.

In addition to the moral complexity presented in modern war films, the prevalence of graphic violence and depictions of warfare's true devastation represent another facet of societal evolution. While earlier films opted for a sanitized vision of war, today's films often choose to confront the audience with the harsh, unfiltered realities of combat. Not only does this conform to a desire for authenticity, but it also manifests the people's rising concerns about the true costs of military conflicts.

Another pivotal point concerns technology's role in warfare and how it is portrayed in cinema. As drones and cyber warfare become more prevalent, films grapple with the disconnect, and sometimes dehumanization, that these remote, mechanized modes of conflict create. As society struggles with these issues, it is unsurprising that they permeate the narratives of war films, encouraging dialogue and critical thought.

War films often represent an avenue for society to come to terms with the aftermath of conflict on the ground. The portrayal of veterans, their struggles, and the often painful process of reintegration reflects society's grappling with the care and understanding owed to these individuals. While filmmakers illuminate these issues, they also force society to confront and engage with them.

This is also true in regards to the subject of civil wars, regional instability, and the refugee crisis. The harrowing journeys, human rights abuses, and global apathy are subjects increasingly tackled in contemporary war films. These narratives reflect society's struggle with empathy, policy formulation, and where to draw the line on sovereignty markers.

Furthermore, the rise of films concerned with intelligence and espionage speaks to society's fascination and dread of clandestine operations and government secrets. Seen less as necessary evils and more as morally grey actions, these stories reflect modern society's nuanced perspective on peace, protection, ethics, and secrecy.

Also, we can't forget how nationalism and patriotism intersect with society's view of modern war. An increase in critical self-reflection, the acceptance of blame, and the acknowledgement of past mistakes in war films show a maturing societal outlook about one's nation and its role in international conflicts. This is a substance, not just style; it signifies society's subconscious wrestling with harsh historical truths.

Therefore, war films serve as society's mirror, reflecting its struggles, realities, and perspectives on modern conflicts. Modern society's interpretation of conflict has evolved, adapting to new realities, reflecting on past mistakes, and explored in nuanced portrayals of war on film.

In this diversification and maturation of societal views on war, cinema plays an essential role. It's a platform which exposes audiences to differing perspectives and realities, confronting viewers with the consequences of conflict that might otherwise seem distant or abstract.

Hence, cinematic representations of conflict function as a vital tool in shaping public discourse. As society continues to grapple with the nature and aftermath of modern wars, films serve not only as a reflection of these discussions but also as a catalyst for deeper and more nuanced understanding.

Modern war films are not just about authenticity or the clangor of battle. They seek to replicate the emotional, moral, and societal complexities associated with contemporary conflict. They challenge our perceptions, make us ask tough questions, and, in the end, foster a more informed society.

By giving voice to diverse perspectives and underscoring the multifaceted nature of modern conflict, war films compel viewers to critically engage with the realities of war. In so doing, they reflect, nurture, and challenge society's concepts and experiences of conflict in the modern world.

Key Films and Genres

The landscape of modern warfare on screen encompasses an extensive array of sub-genres and significant movies that explore various aspects of war experiences. It's intriguing to analyze how this assortment of motion pictures has effectively depicted the changing dynamics of warfare over time.

The genre of 'anti-war films' is a pertinent category. Essentially, these films underline the brutality and senselessness of conflicts with the intention of discouraging glorification of warfare. Stanley Kubrick's 'Paths of Glory' (1957) and Oliver Stone's 'Platoon' (1986) exemplify narrative arcs that favor the human spirit over bombastic war depictions.

Alongside classic anti-war films, 'combat films' deserve special mention. While these films don't necessarily glorify combat, they offer an intensively realistic depiction of battlefield conditions. Steven Spielberg's 'Saving Private Ryan' (1998) attempts to do exactly that, with its sharp D-Day landing sequence that stands as a paradigm of gritty realism in combat scenes.

'War dramas' also play a crucial role. These films focus more on the personal narratives of characters in war, often highlighting the emotional toll of warfare, as seen in 'The Thin Red Line' (1998) by Terrence Malick. Likewise, war romances like 'Casablanca' (1942) show the ways in which war impacts personal relationships and human interaction in general.

Another fundamental genre is 'war-time adventure films'. These narratives focus on grand war-time escapades, rich in thrills and excitement. Memorable films in this category include 'The Great Escape' (1963) and 'Where Eagles Dare' (1968).

Moreover, 'political war films' explore the geopolitical complexities of war while offering a critique of the decision-making processes involved in warfare. Movies like 'Dr.

Strangelove or: How I Learned to Stop Worrying and Love the Bomb' (1964) offer a satirical examination of Cold War policies. On the other hand, 'The Deer Hunter' (1978) delves into the impact of political decisions on individuals affected by the Vietnam War.

'War comedies' form an absorbing subset, combining humor with the grim realities of war. Movies like 'M*A*S*H' (1970) or 'Catch-22' (1970) have used humor as an effective tool to expose the absurdities of war.

Apart from these, 'war epics' have generated considerable interest owing to their grand scale narrative arcs that often cover extensive periods. Examples include 'Lawrence of Arabia' (1962) which tells the tale of a British officer's experiences in the Arabian Peninsula during World War I.

Moving beyond traditional warfare, 'nuclear war films' like 'The Day After' (1983) open up a new arena focusing on nuclear anxieties. Similarly, films dealing with ongoing conflicts such as the Iraq War form another remarkable genre, with films like 'The Hurt Locker' (2008), which examines the realities of bomb disposal teams.

The genre of 'war documentaries' also merits attention, exemplified by docudramas like 'The Fog of War: Eleventh Lessons from the Life of Robert S. McNamara' (2003), which offers an insight into the complexities and enigmas of war, as narrated by a former Defense Secretary.

The sub-genre of 'wartime resistance movies' adds another dimension to the portrayal of heroism during war. Films like 'Schindler's List' (1993) tell inspiring tales of courage that unfolded away from the battlefield.

'War crime films' dig deeper into the controversy and inhuman acts associated with warfare, often leading to impactful narratives like 'Judgment at Nuremberg' (1961), which revolves around war trials post World War II.

Last but not least, 'Prisoner of War (POW) films' deal with the experiences of battlefield prisoners in enemy camps. This genre includes films like 'The Bridge on the River Kwai' (1957) and 'Stalag 17' (1953) which surface the hardships and struggles faced by POWs.

In conclusion, the diversity and richness of the war movie genre reflects the many facets of human experiences in times of war. The influences these films have had on shaping public perceptions of war cannot be overlooked. While we marvel at the creatively portrayed narratives, we also realize how the celluloid battlefield is a mirror to the world's geopolitical evolution, past and present.

Chapter 7: The Impact of War Films on Veterans

Delving into the influence of war films on those who have faced combat's raw grit and grim reality, we find an intertwining narrative of solace, reflection and, at times, painful reminders. The depiction of soldiers on the silver screen – their bravery, camaraderie, losses, and sacrifices – can resonate deeply with veterans, offering them a gateway to open conversations about their experiences or providing an echo of their untold stories. It's not uncommon to find that films, even ones born from fictional narratives, can act as a mirror for veterans, reflecting their own struggles and facilitating personal healing or catharsis from their often unspoken trauma. The power of cinema can extend beyond mere representation; it sparks dialogues and fosters understanding, bridging the gap between the battlefield and home front. A poignant yet unequivocal aspect of this is the involvement of veterans in film production. Their hands-on roles as consultants, actors, or even directors ensure authentic storytelling, while providing a therapeutic outlet and meaningful post-service careers. Navigating the journey towards understanding veteran experiences is no mere stroll down memory lane; rather, it's an exploration into the war-battered human psyche and the continual search for resilience and redemption.

Cinematic Representation of Soldiers

As the narrative transitions from one epoch of war films to another, it's hard to overlook the varying representations of soldiers throughout the different eras of filmmaking. From stereotypical caricatures to complex characters struggling with the consequences of war, the cinematic portrayal of soldiers has evolved dramatically.

During the early years of war films, soldiers were often depicted as one-dimensional characters. The narrative focus was primarily on the battles and strategic developments. Consequently, the individual soldier's personal narrative was more or less ignored. The emphasis was heavily tilted towards larger-than-life personalities, often generically upbeat and patriotic heroes who were viewed as glamorous even in the face of war.

There were reasons why filmmakers avoided the real behind-the-lines narrative. It was a time when cinema and society were both in their relative infancy in dealing with the disaster of war. There was also a societal need to romanticize the role of the soldier to make the sacrifice bearable.

The cinematic representation of soldiers started to evolve during the Cold War period. Film festivals began showing darker, more complex takes on soldiers caught in the machinations of political power games. Movies like "Paths of Glory" challenge the viewer's comfort zone, revealing that beneath the uniform, there lies a person with fears, dreams, and personal battles.

Often it is the harshness of conflict itself forcing a breakdown in the stereotypical facade of the soldier, unveiling a reality that is morally murky at best. This was a significant departure from the black and white opponents of earlier war films, providing a more humanistic lens through which the audience could understand the soldier.

As cinema entered the era of the Vietnam War, the depiction of soldiers underwent a revolution. The young recruit, the disillusioned veteran, the haunted survivor - these became the staple characters of Vietnam War films. Demystifying the heroic ideal, these films tackled issues of mental health, disillusion, and moral crisis soldiers were grappling with.

What followed is a noticeable shift in the representation of soldiers. War films began to introduce nuances and complexities to their characters. The soldiers were no longer considered just war machines, but as human beings caught in the crossfire. This reflected a society's changing view on war and the individuals who fight them.

Modern war movies continue this trend of in-depth characterization. War is messy, and so are the lives of the soldiers caught in them. You'll find characters battling with PTSD, losing loved ones, and dealing with societal alienation. Cinematic representation of soldiers has shifted from being a romantic and glorified image, towards a more accurate and often heartbreaking depiction of the reality of those who serve.

The film "American Sniper", for instance, showcases the harsh realities of the modern military experience, emphasizing the physical, emotional, and psychological toll war takes on soldiers and their families. Unlike films of the past that focused predominantly on the battlefield, it delves into the soldier's life, his homecoming, and his struggles with everyday life after his duty is over.

Now that the filmmakers are more willingly exploring the darker corners of the conflict, we see an increased emphasis on moral ambiguity. The line which separates the heroes from villains in the war movies has gradually been blurred. It is cinema reflecting on reality, taking it upon themselves to question the 'justness' of war and to explore the heavy toll it takes on the human psyche.

The multi-faceted portrayal of soldiers in cinema is indicative of our evolving cultural perception of war and those who partake in it. War is no longer romanticized to the degree that it once was. The narrative now centers around ordinary people thrown into extraordinary circumstances, and how it changes them forever.

The cinematic representation of soldiers serves as a mirror to society. It has become a platform to express the unspeakable, to enlighten the audience about the harsh realities of war, and the psychological burden carried by those who fight it.

Conclusively, war movies have evolved from platforms of propaganda and heroic myth-making to in-depth character studies. The transformation in the depiction of soldiers is evidence of that. With increasing societal introspection about the nature of war, the future of war films is likely to delve even deeper into the physical and psychological landscapes that characterize the life of soldiers. This shift holds the promise of greater empathy and understanding towards those who serve.

Healing and Trauma through Film

Our journey to comprehend the transformative power of cinema now leads us to explore how war films can serve as extraordinary pathways to healing and understanding trauma. When handled with sensitivity and insight, the genre can illuminate profound human experiences, create empathetic spaces, and, in the process, foster healing.

Imagination is as much a battlefield as reality is, if not more so. The visceral imagery and emotional narratives that cinema provides can manifest itself as a form of catharsis for the audience, and especially, war veterans. War movies can bring suppressed memories to the surface, prompting confronting, discussing, and understanding the traumas faced in war. This catharsis, while potentially painful initially, can be a crucial first step towards healing.

Moreover, watching war films can conveniently create a platform for veterans to engage in conversations about their experiences. For many of these combat veterans, speaking about what they've been through can be tremendously challenging. Cinema provides a form of release and enables the articulation of the sensations felt but seldom expressed.

War films can serve as educational tools that relay the horrors of war to a wider audience, encouraging understanding and empathy. It's through this shared consciousness that society becomes more attuned to the sacrifice of veterans and the weight of their lived experiences. In this sense, war films contribute to healing on an individual level and bring about a societal transformation grounded in compassion and comprehension.

Historically, war movies have been instrumental in de-stigmatizing the psychological injuries soldiers wrestle with long after battles have concluded. They have effectively familiarized audiences with conditions such as post-traumatic stress disorder (PTSD), helping people understand that it's not a sign of weakness but a natural response to excessive stress and horror.

This demystification is crucial in healing the unseen wounds left by war. By creating an atmosphere of acceptance and understanding, society encourages veterans to seek help, moving closer to reconciliation and recovery.

However, the capacity of war films to heal is not one-dimensional. The art form has also contributed significantly by providing veterans with a channel for perspective-taking, especially when they contribute to the film production process. Being behind the camera can be just as poignant as being in front of it.

Capturing the raw essence of war can be cathartic for veterans themselves, taking them on a journey of self-understanding and healing. Creating the narrative allows control over their past experiences, providing a sense of power that can be therapeutic.

While cinema can often embellish and dramatize, the creators responsible for these war narratives also need to approach their subjects with just as much sensitivity as their audience. Authentic representation is the key in this case. The point isn't to re-traumatize the audience or the veterans portrayed but to draw attention to their stories, providing them a voice they might not have had otherwise.

Telling their stories can give veterans the agency to rewrite their personal narrative surrounding the war, displacing the trauma with a story of resilience and survival. Transforming the experience from a negative to a positive can have profound healing implications, both for the individual and the audience bearing witness.

That said, filmmakers must remain vigilant in their mission to portray war responsibly. Misrepresentation can lead to harmful stereotypes, further alienating audiences from the realities of those who've experienced war first-hand. The healing potential of war films can only be unlocked when the stories are told with nuance, honesty, and respect for those that have been there.

Furthermore, the inclusion of multidimensional characters in war films treads the path of holistic representation, contributing to the healing process. By presenting characters in a multitude of roles - as warriors, as victims, as healers - filmmakers can create diverse narratives that resonate with a broader audience, fostering understanding, empathy, and healing.

In conclusion, cinema possesses the power to provide solace, inspire conversations, break stigmas, and support collective healing. However, this power comes with an obligation to tell stories responsibly and respectfully. As we navigate the narratives of war, the compassionate lens of cinema illuminates the path, reminding us that healing is not only about forgetting or moving on, but also about remembering, understanding, and above all, empathizing.

The remainder of this book will explore how war films continue to evolve and challenge societal norms, first delving into the representation of women and minorities in these films, and then investigating the thorny ethical issues that surround war filmmaking. As we navigate this exploration, remember, cinema shapes and reflects our lives in extraordinary ways, and its beautiful, tumultuous magic continues to leave imprints on our hearts and minds.

Veterans in Film Production

War films have a profound impact on many of our lives, but the individuals most affected by these narratives are often those who lived through these events first hand: the veterans. With their rich, firsthand experiences, many veterans have moved past the roles of mere consumers of war movies and become active participants in the filmmaking process. This chapter will look at the unique impacts and contributions of these veterans in film production.

Veterans bring a unique depth of understanding and authenticity to war films. Their insights don't just extend to the large-scale strategic elements, but also the nuanced details which only someone who has served can truly understand. The resultant effects aren't just limited to the screen; they often play sizable roles in script adjustments, set designs, character development, and more, contributing to a more grounded and realistic portrayal of war.

Yet, it isn't just about credibility or authenticity. Veterans in film production often have a profound sense of responsibility to their fallen comrades, to tell their stories with respect and honesty. This leads to careful deliberations over the narrative representation and overall filmic attitude towards the subject matter. There is a deep-seated determination to ensure that the sacrifices and experiences of their brothers and sisters in arms are depicted with the depth and nuance they deserve.

One might wonder if a veteran's involvement in war films triggers memories of traumatic experiences. It can indeed, and this sort of therapeutic confrontation is often a part of the intention. Conversion of trauma into a creative process can be a cathartic and healing experience. It allows these veterans to give their raw emotions a voice, validating them in a way that translates into compelling cinema.

Given the nature of the subject matter, war films are bound to be political. Veterans in film production can provide a balanced view on warfare. Their firsthand experiences coupled with an understanding of the associated trauma can lead to a fairer and less glamorized depiction of war.

Beyond serving as consultants or advisors, many veterans have found their calling as directors, producers, or writers in the film industry. They bring their personal experiences to bear, adding a palpable realism to the narrative that resonates deeply with viewers.

As actors, veterans' familiarity with military life can contribute an authenticity to their on-screen representations. From the weary resolve of a seasoned soldier to the jarring upheaval of a new recruit, their performances can become embodiments of relatable human experience rather than a dramatized spectacle.

There is a growing trend in Hollywood to include veterans in the filmmaking process. This initiative not only ensures a realistic portrayal of warfare but also provides veterans with opportunities beyond the military. Through film production, they're empowered to channel their experiences into creative endeavors and contribute to a larger dialogue about war and its effects.

Despite these valuable contributions, the involvement of veterans in film production also sparks critical questions. How does their involvement influence the depiction of war? Can a veteran's perspective unintentionally propagate or reinforce harmful stereotypes or misconceptions about warfare? These considerations have to be made to ensure that movies do not end up glorifying war or oversimplifying its complexities.

Further, even if their involvement enhances the accuracy of the film, it may still fall short of the lived reality. War is brutal, messy, and defies tidy narratives. Therefore, striking a balance between realism and viewer discretion is an art, one that needs to be continually refined.

In conclusion, veterans offer an invaluable perspective to the film industry when it comes to war films. Their experience and knowledge add a layer of authenticity and depth to these films, and their involvement can serve as a healing process for them. However, it is essential to tread carefully to avoid misrepresentation or oversimplification of the subject matter.

Film is the mirror that reflects our society and shapes our perceptions, and veterans have a crucial role to play in this discourse. Their involvement in film production not only shapes the narratives woven on-screen but also the discussions these stories spur off-screen. So, the next time we watch a war film, let's remember that the flickering images before us might well be the encapsulation of a veteran's reality, retold with an intent to enlighten, inspire, and remember.

We owe it to these veterans and all those who have experienced war to listen carefully, ask informed questions, and engage with these narratives critically. By doing so, we not only honor their service but also contribute to a more nuanced and informed understanding of warfare and its impacts on human lives.

In the next chapter, we'll explore the roles and representations of women and minorities in war films. These demographic groups have experienced warfare and its repercussions uniquely, and that provides more diverse narratives to explore.

Chapter 8: Women and Minorities in War Films

The intersection of war films with the narratives of women and minorities takes us down an inspiring lane of metamorphosis that set the foundations for socio-political change, both on and off the screen. Once relegated to ancillary roles or stereotyped portrayals, the gradual shift towards authentic and inclusive representation mirrored society's grappling with issues of sexism and discrimination. Character arcs for women evolved from passive bystanders or mirrors of men's valor towards complex, courageous figures battling adversity in their own right. Such trailblazing transformations within the genre brought forth pioneering films like "Sophie Scholl: The Final Days" and "A League of Their Own." Staunch racial and ethnic stereotypes were challenged, giving way to the dignified representation of minorities. The revolutionary impact of movies like "Glory" and "Windtalkers," demonstrating the valor of African-American and Native American soldiers respectively, can't be underestimated. The world of war films thus became a platform for essential social commentary, subtly arousing awareness and empathy within audiences towards these marginalized communities, initiating constructive conversations around equality and justice.

Changing Roles and Representations

The war film genre, along with the rest of the film industry, has seen a significant shift in roles and representations over the years. The formerly male-centered industry with a single lens perspective has gradually made space for diverse voices and more complex portrayals of participants in war. This transformation became particularly noticeable in the late 20th and early 21st century, time periods notable for multitudinous global changes such as strides in women's rights and racial equality.

Women, initially relegated to the roles of nurses, mothers, wives or love interests, saw a dramatic shift in the war film genre. Filmmakers began to write them into the narrative in more integral and layered roles. For example, "Courage Under Fire" (1996) starred Meg Ryan as a helicopter pilot and officer in the US Army brought under scrutiny for her actions during Operation Desert Storm. Ryan's character not only fought in combat but is posthumously considered for the Medal of Honor, marking a crucial turning point in representation.

Also noteworthy is "Zero Dark Thirty" (2012), a film revolving around the hunt for Osama Bin Laden, led by a female CIA analyst. The film boldly put women into the forefront of military strategy and combat, illustrating their evolving roles in modern warfare. "Zero Dark Thirty" portrayed a female-centric perspective of the war, a rarity in the genre.

Another zenith of changing representation in war films prominently involves racial and ethnic minority groups. Representation of African-American soldiers in particular, although initially fraught with stereotypes or underrepresentation, began to expand and evolve. The 1989 film "Glory" stands out in this regard. It narrates the story of an all-black volunteer regiment during the Civil War, spotlighting the bravery and sacrifices of these soldiers who were rarely acknowledged in earlier war films.

"Windtalkers" (2002) shone a light on the Navajo Tribe's contributions to the World War II efforts as their native language was used for secure military communications. The film showcased an essential yet overlooked aspect of the Native American contribution to the war effort, highlighting their heroism and patriotism despite racial discrimination at home.

Equally significant has been the cinematic evolution in representing soldiers' identity in terms of sexuality. Although a still-infrequent occurrence, films such as "A Single Man" (2009) and "Milk" (2008) have begun to incorporate narratives that explore the intersection of warfare and LGBTQ+ experiences.

In the realm of characters with disabilities, "Born on the Fourth of July" (1989), brought to life the pre-and post-war experiences of Ron Kovic, a paralyzed Vietnam War veteran. It underscored the physical and emotional struggles of disabled veterans, their fight for recognition, and their struggles for equal treatment.

The war film genre has also delved into the mental health side of warfare with films acknowledging post-traumatic stress disorder (PTSD), often overlooked in early films of the genre. "The Deer Hunter" (1978) and "American Sniper" (2014), for instance, brought this issue directly into the public eye.

Even the nature of warfare itself has seen a shift in representation. Filmmakers have broadened the genre's scope beyond traditional battlefield engagements, introducing covert operations, cyber warfare, and terrorism as new themes. Films like "Black Hawk Down" (2001) and "The Hurt Locker" (2009) have been instrumental in depicting the shift from traditional warfare to modern, complex military operations.

Moving forward, the diversity in representation and storytelling will continue to shape the landscape of war films, with an increasing emphasis on authenticity and inclusivity. More attention will be paid to marginalized groups in war - whether on the home front or the battlefield, expanding the narrative beyond the conventional.

While strides have been made, there remains a long journey toward accurate and balanced representation in war films. For certain marginalized groups (like trans and non-binary people), representation is still minimal to non-existent. Furthermore, the intersection of identities is severely lacking. Consideration of these nuances will contribute to a more detailed tapestry of the war narrative, truthfully capturing its collective and inclusive nature.

The change in roles and representations in war films holds a mirror up to society's evolution and serves as a reminder that although war is deeply entrenched in human history, our understanding and interpretation of it are bound by our cultural context. This cultural context is ever-changing, and our films must shift to accurately reflect this reality.

Breakthrough Films and Characters

War films have long been dominated by the male perspective, traditionally showcasing these characters as the heroic figures leading combat. This has given rise to iconic characters such as Tom Hanks' Captain John Miller in 'Saving Private Ryan', Martin Sheen's Benjamin Willard in 'Apocalypse Now', and the likes. However, as societal views evolved, so too has the representation of characters in war films, giving us breakthrough films that have dared to break this mold.

'Casablanca,' an unforgettable drama set during WWII, introduced us to the complex character of Ilsa Lund, portrayed by Ingrid Bergman. Lund is an intriguing character, a woman caught between love and duty, whose decisions rapidly shape the narrative. An iconic character who defied the damsel-in-distress stereotype, she represented a shift in storytelling in war films.

Precursors to later breakthrough films, 'Casablanca' and others like it were not just films with female leads, but powerful narratives that emphasized their agency and capacity to drive the plot beyond romantic subplots. Women were no longer merely a love interest or a cause for men to fight, but active participants in the events unfolding.

Progress was slow, but a steady stream of films began to further challenge the status quo. A turning point came in 1986 with 'Platoon,' which, unlike previous films, focused on the experiences of a grunt-level soldier instead of a heroic officer, shedding light on the realities faced by average soldiers.

The 2001 film 'Enemy at the Gates' offered another innovative approach by focusing on a Russian sniper during the Battle of Stalingrad, an unusual departure from the Western-centric narratives of traditional WWII films. This change of lens underscored the universal trauma of war, regardless of nationality or rank.

Small strides in racial diversity were made in war films like 'Glory' and 'Tuskegee Airmen.' 'Glory' is a landmark film that showcased the bravery and sacrifice of African-American soldiers during the Civil War, humanizing these characters who had often been marginalized in past films. Similarly, 'Tuskegee Airmen' chronicles the experiences of the first African-American military aviators in the U.S. Armed Forces.

Moving into the 21st century, war films began to further challenge traditional boundaries. 'Jarhead', released in 2005, was lauded for its authenticity and unflinching portrayal of the mental and physical hardships faced by U.S. Marines during the first Gulf War. The film's open discussion of the psychological impact of wars would pave the way for future films exploring this theme.

In recent years, films like 'Beasts of No Nation' and 'The Breadwinner' have expanded the genre further by focusing on child soldiers and victims of war, thus presenting a haunting perspective that is frequently overlooked. These films have provoked thoughtful discussions about the devastating and far-reaching toll that war leaves in its wake.

While not a war film in the traditional sense, 'Hidden Figures' is noteworthy for showcasing the role of African American women who were instrumental in NASA's efforts during the Space Race, which was a direct byproduct of the Cold War. This film is essential for its contributions to amplifying the oft-overshadowed perspectives in war narratives.

Diversity in the representation of lesbian, gay, bisexual, transgender, and queer (LGBTQ+) characters in war films has also gradually improved. 'The Imitation Game,' a biopic about British mathematician and WWII codebreaker Alan Turing, acknowledges his homosexuality openly. This nuanced integration of LGBTQ+ narratives in war films is a recent development that signals increasing inclusivity within the genre.

'Zero Dark Thirty', a modern war film primarily about the hunt for Osama bin Laden, is led by Jessica Chastain's character, Maya. It's rare to see a woman leading such a mission in a war film, representing a shift in narrative and challenging the preconceived notion of gender roles within this genre.

In this evolution of characters and narratives, we must also recognize films such as 'Full Metal Jacket' and 'Apocalypse Now' that pushed boundaries not by changing who the main characters were, but by exploring the depths of their psychological torments, depicting them as victims of a dehumanizing system rather than solitary heroes. This psychological exploration allowed a deeper level of engagement and empathy for these characters.

In conclusion, while a lot of progress has been made in terms of representation in war films, there is still much room for improvement. With the growing recognition of marginalized voices and stories, we can hope to see more films and characters that reflect the true diversity of experiences in war.

And yet, the challenges persist. Despite the increasing awareness and portrayal of diverse characters and themes, war films continue to be dominated by Western narratives. As audiences, historians, and film students, we must push for and support narratives from diverse perspectives. It is by incorporating these unique experiences that the genre can evolve and continue to influence and educate audiences about the many facets of war.

Social Commentary through Cinema

Although war movies may seem removed from everyday life, they, like all other forms of art, are a reflection of the culture and society they were created in. Many war films are known to push boundaries, ask moral questions, and offer social commentary. Through strong characters, controversial themes, and powerful narratives, these films provoke the audience's understanding of socio-political issues surrounding war and conflict.

One way that social commentary comes to life in war films is through the representation of the common soldiers. These characters are often showcased as ordinary members of society who are propelled into an extraordinary, often inhuman, situation. Be it an anxious private in "Saving Private Ryan", a complaisant Captain in "Apocalypse Now," or a stubborn colonel in "Platoon," the characters' experiences and transformations offer sharp criticisms of war's devastating impacts.

Most significantly, war films provide a platform to challenge and attack practices or policies that are unjust. Movies like "Dr. Strangelove" satirically portrayed a dysfunctional government in the Cold War era. Similarly, "Paths of Glory" offered a damning indictment of the military bureaucracy of World War I, condemning the exploitation and senseless sacrifice of soldiers for the sake of pride or strategy.

At times, war films take a step further and debate specific societal norms and mores. "The Deer Hunter", a film set amid the Vietnam war, used the platform to comment on the blue-collar struggles in America and the individuals' loss of innocence and humanity due to war. Likewise, "Three Kings", a film about the first Gulf War, critiqued American consumerism and materialism represented through the soldiers' pursuit of hidden gold.

Furthermore, war films often shape discourse over issues of nationalism and patriotism. For instance, films like "Full

Metal Jacket" and "Apocalypse Now" typically portray war as a dehumanizing process, debunking the heroism attached to nationalistic sentiments. Whereas films like "American Sniper" lean into patriotic narratives, though not without their own shades of critique and complexity.

Moreover, films about war also make statements about gender roles, race, and class inequalities in society. The changes in the roles and representations of women and minorities have been especially noteworthy. In the film "A Few Good Men", a female military lawyer's struggles to prove herself in a male-dominated field expose systemic sexism and gender bias. Films like "Glory" have also highlighted the discrimination and racism faced by African American soldiers.

The issue of PTSD (Post Traumatic Stress Disorder) among veterans is another significant theme encountered in war films. "Born on the Fourth of July" and "The Hurt Locker" are honest portrayals of the physical and mental trauma soldiers face when they return home from war. These films allow for a broader discussion about combat stress and, in turn, challenge the society's responsibility towards veterans.

War films have also portrayed the changing dynamics of warfare in the modern age, including the rise of terrorism, drone warfare, and cyber warfare. Films like "Zero Dark Thirty" and "Eye in the Sky" critically engage with the morals, ethics, and legality of these newer forms of conflict.

In addition, by depicting conflicts in various parts of the world, war films can bring global issues into the limelight. They have often catalyzed discussions about foreign policy and intervention, challenging the audience's perception of 'us vs. them'. "Black Hawk Down" and "Hotel Rwanda", for instance, confront viewers with the harsh realities of international conflicts and genocides.

However, it's essential to consider that although war films provide social commentary, their views are not always universally agreed upon. These films are often subjects of vigorous debates and controversies regarding their portrayal of historical events, racial or gender representation, or the glorification of violence and war.

Furthermore, the influence of these commentaries can vary drastically depending upon cultural, geopolitical, and temporal contexts. Different audiences may interpret the same film in different ways based on their personal experiences, societal norms, or political beliefs.

Yet, regardless of the controversies and debates surrounding them, war films act as important cultural artifacts; they challenge perceptions, incite discussions, and reflect societal sentiments. They are a tool for both the filmmakers and the audience to understand and interpret the world we live in and the socio-political conflicts that mold it.

From this perspective, war films are not just an entertainment medium but an influential force in shaping social narratives. They challenge, critique, and comment on society, making us reflect on the human cost of conflict and the complexity of the world we inhabit.

As we progress into the subsequent chapters of this book, we will explore more nuanced aspects of these commentaries, with a particular focus on the ethics of war filmmaking and the future of war films. Understanding the riveting dynamic of social commentary in cinema is instrumental in situating war films in society's collective consciousness.

Chapter 9: The Ethics of War Filmmaking

Having traversed the landscapes of stylistic and social evolution in war films, understanding the ethics of war filmmaking stands as a crucial component in this exploration. Filmmakers often tread the precarious path between artistry and propriety, tasked with capturing elaborate and emotion-driven narratives without trivializing the horrific realities of war. The creation of these films often stirs controversy; critics may argue certain portrayals are unnecessary, exploitative, or even propagandistic. What's more, some say that the commodification of war could risk desensitizing audiences to the true brutality of battle. But it's essential to remember a paramount debate in the film industry: the critical balance between the freedom to craft poignant, thought-provoking art and the responsibility to respect and acknowledge the tragedy of violent conflict. This delicate dance of art and sensitivity dominate the discussions of ethics in war filmmaking, leading us to an introspective observation of the medium's possible implications and the continuing conversation surrounding its refinement.

Balancing Art and Sensitivity

Creating war films is accompanied by a significant responsibility; sometimes the artistic intention clashes with the need for sensitivity, especially when the subject matter is grounded in realities that have deeply affected millions of lives. In war films, this tension is often apparent, as directors must balance the desire to tell a compelling story with the need to truthfully depict the harrowing realities of war.

Steven Spielberg's film "Saving Private Ryan" offers a perfect example of this delicate negotiation. The film's infamous opening scene, portraying the D-day landings, has been praised for its brutal yet sensitive portrayal of the horrors faced by soldiers. The director's artful approach towards uncompromising realism served as a respectful acknowledgment of the soldiers' lived experiences, avoiding the glorification of violence.

However, filmmakers need to be aware that a strong commitment to realism does not give license for gratuitous violence. The sincerity of the story is compromised when the portrayal of violence becomes excessive and sensationalized. This point is evident in Oliver Stone's "Platoon," where the violence is raw and undeniably disturbing, yet its necessity to the story keeps it from becoming gratuitous, thereby maintaining the film's integrity.

Accuracy is another pillar in sensitively presenting war. The war film "Black Hawk Down," though artfully crafted, faced criticism for factual inaccuracies. Despite delivering a thrilling visual spectacle, the film's lack of adherence to real-life events indicated a break from sensitivity toward the people and events being portrayed.

The award-winning film "The Hurt Locker," though lauded for its intense storytelling, attracted similar criticism. While the film offered a nerve-wracking firefight depiction within the Iraq war context, many veterans expressed disappointment over its inaccurate representation of soldier behavior and military protocols. Sensitivity must prevail over art in such instances, ensuring that films do not undermine or corrupt actual experiences for the sake of drama.

Balancing art and sensitivity also requires consideration of the cultural and historical context of the war being portrayed. "Apocalypse Now," for instance, misses this mark. While the film succeeds in artistically displaying the breakdown of human morality, it falls short in its sensitive portrayal of Vietnamese people and their experiences, thus failing the delicate balancing act.

Equally challenging is handling sensitive war-related themes, like genocide, with the necessary degree of respect and responsibility. Film directors strive not to smudge the harsh lines of historical reality, and films like "Schindler's List" testify to this principle. Spielberg's approach to shooting the film entirely in black and white draws viewers into a stylized narrative without mitigating the atrocities presented.

Likewise, "The Pianist" tackles the sensitive theme of holocaust with striking reverence. Director Roman Polanski did not merely rely on the art of filmmaking, but delicately engraved sensitivity into each frame, resulting in a film that is both beautifully made and respectful of the historical horrors it portrays.

At times, filmmakers may choose to balance art and sensitivity through the reframing of perspectives, focussing not on the war itself but on its impact on individuals and communities. Terrence Malick's "A Thin Red Line" is a notable example, highlighting the psychological impact of war on soldiers.

Films that offer a reflection on the trauma of war rather than the spectacle of war such as "Coming Home" and "Born on the Fourth of July," resonate with audiences by centering on the human side of war. These films manage to masterfully balance artistic value and sensitivity, thus underscoring the necessity of this balance in creating meaningful cinema.

In sum, balancing art and sensitivity in war films is a tightrope walk for filmmakers, teetering between cinematic aesthetics and moral responsibility for accurate, sensitive portrayals. War films have the unique potential to inform audiences about the realities of war while delivering a compelling narrative. If balanced correctly, the film can serve as a bridge connecting the past, the present, and the myriad human experiences shaped by war.

Controversy and Criticism

War movies have been mired in controversy from the outset. The debate often revolves around the question of verisimilitude, the balance between art and historical accuracy, and the ethical issues associated with retelling violent and traumatizing events.

One of the longstanding criticisms of war films is their potential to romanticize and glamorize war. While filmmakers confer narrative structure upon their war stories to engage the audience, it's important to remember that real war is messy, chaotic, and devoid of narrative resolution. For instance, some critics argue that iconic war films like "Saving Private Ryan" or "The Hurt Locker" oversimplify complex geopolitical situations that initiate wars. Others claim that they glorify violent actions and even perpetuate a warrior mythos by building stories around heroic, seemingly invincible soldiers.

The selective portrayal of war, often through a narrow lens, is another point of contention. Historically, war films have disproportionately highlighted stories from a Eurocentric or American context. As a result, the atrocities and sacrifices of non-Western soldiers and civilians are often overlooked. This bias not only distorts our understanding of global conflicts, but also perpetuates a narrative that positions Western nations as the saviors.

The depiction of violence in war films is a subject of intense debate. Film theorists argue that gratuitous violence often distracts from the message of the film and dehumanizes the enemy. At the same time, films that shy away from showing the horrors of war may be accused of sanitizing reality, thereby reducing the gravity and tragedy associated with warfare.

Another sphere of controversy is the manner in which veterans are portrayed. There's a perennial question: does the depiction of veterans in war films contribute to or alleviate the stigmatization of veteran trauma? For every film that confronts PTSD and the adjustment to civilian life, there are those that stereotype veterans as unstable or unfit for society. Navigating the fine line between representation and exploitation is a recurring struggle.

War films dealing with recent or ongoing conflicts are often criticized for their political bias. These films present an opportunity to shape public perception, and critics worry that twisting facts or propagating one-sided narratives may lead to distortion of the truth and social discord. Concerns about propaganda were particularly pronounced during the World Wars and the Cold War, where cinema became a tool to sway public sentiment.

Interestingly, some criticism stems from factual errors or anachronisms, which are often unavoidable given the complexity of history and the constraints of filmmaking. However, critics argue that these deviations from truth can affect the validity of the film's message, especially if the inaccuracies play into stereotypes or outdated beliefs.

The representation of women and minorities in war films is subject to scrutiny. Critics argue that erasing or marginalizing these individuals in narratives can reinforce harmful stereotypes and pigeonholing. At its worst, it ignores the heroics and sacrifices of these groups and discredits their contributions to the war effort.

Moreover, critics often chastise war films for romanticizing the notion of sacrifice. By celebrating heroic endure and selfless acts without dwelling on the needless loss and human cost, these films can perpetuate a desensitized view of warfare.

Censorship rules of different countries also come into play. These regulations heavily influence how conflicts are depicted. Consequently, filmmakers sway between the urge to assert artistic freedom and the need to conform to restrictive norms.

Even though war movies are a means of memorializing and reflecting on conflicts, they inevitably fall short due to the sheer magnitude and complexity of wartime experiences. Some critics posit that any attempt to recreate these experiences is futile and undermines the gravitas of war.

The final concern, particularly relevant in today's interconnected world, is that of cultural sensitivity. When filmmakers represent foreign cultures or conflicts, there is a responsibility to approach with nuance and understanding to avoid perpetuating harmful stereotypes and cultural misunderstandings.

In summary, war films, despite their power and impact, are fraught with controversy regarding their depiction of war, those who fight, and the societies caught in the fray. The balance between reality, entertainment, and ethical representation is an ongoing debate that encapsulates broader societal conversations about the role and scope of cinema.

In the end, it is crucial to watch war films with a discerning eye and question the narratives presented. Engaging critically with these films allows us to learn from the past while remaining open to nuanced interpretations of history and human experience.

Ethical Debates and Discussions

When delving into the intricate world of war filmography, a multifaceted web of ethical matters comes forth. No facet of cinema induces such discussions more ardently than war films. It's an all-encompassing narrative, going beyond the screen's boundaries, questioning societal norms and preconceived beliefs about war and its depiction.

At the very root, these ethical debates are about the fine line between respect for real-world scenarios and realities, and the creation of entertainment, while steering clear of glorification. It's a delicate process. It begs the question of how much truth should be represented and how these truths should be depicted. This chapter delves into these ethical dilemmas in detail, juxtaposing the artistic representation of war alongside its respects for the harsh realities.

Realism is perhaps the most critical debate in war films. Is there a palpable need for explicit violence, or are the horrors of war best left to the viewers' imagination? Material steeped in an excess of visceral content often fuels debates on how much realism is too much. Critics argue such extremes could actually be a form of voyeurism sitting uncomfortably at the intersection of entertainment and human suffering.

A similar ethical question revolves around the depiction of the individuals involved in war. The haunted, heroic soldier, often glorified, is a common figure in such films. But not all who go to war experience the same realities. And then there's the question of juxtaposing the individual against the horrors of war. How do these portrayals impact the psyche of veterans who have experienced war first hand?

There is a secondary layer to this - the enemy's portrayal. It's a delicate narrative switch, one that can easily cross into the realm of stereotyping and racial profiling. The depiction of the opponents in such situations becomes a matter of significant ethical concern; heightening an atmosphere of already mounting tensions.

Then comes the issue of censorship versus freedom of expression. War films are often subject to a stringent screening process before being released to public screenings. This raises questions about where to draw the line between sanitizing content for public consumption and providing an authentic representation of war's atrocities. How much truth ought to be sacrificed in the name of public decorum, and yet not paint an unreal image of war?

Cultural sensitivity plays a prominent role in the discussion of ethical filmmaking. While some films honor cultural sensitivities, others fall flat, leading to heated debates over ethnocentrism and cultural stereotyping. Film studios grapple with ensuring respectful presentation of diverse cultures and maintaining engaging plots.

On a more philosophical level, the ethical debate also examines the role of war films in society. Do these movies merely mirror realities, or do they subtly encourage violent inclinations? How do we treat war films - as spectacles of violence or as cautionary tales against the horrors of warfare?

There is a transforming dimension of time to consider within these ethics too. As society changes, so do its cultural shifts, and its perceptions on various themes in art, including war. Past films, that might have acquitted themselves well on the ethical front at the time of their release, may not hold up by today's evolved standards.

The discussions on the ethics of war filmmaking are vast, intense, and complex. No one-size-fits-all answer exists. It is a constant dialogue, changing and evolving, just as cinema and society do over time. As filmmakers, we need to keep an ear to the ground with these dialogues, being sensitive to them so we can better utilize our craft. This conversational loop is a part of a constant push and pull, helping cinema, particularly war films, steadily evolve.

The goal is to present war not as a glorified spectacle, but rather as a humane narrative. Balancing the scales between entertainment, artistry, and moral sensitivity is the tricky part. Graduate from the common clichés; embrace the depth of human emotion; respect the enormity and complexity of war and its effects - That's how we could perhaps attempt to bring some clarity into this ethical maze that is war filmmaking.

At the end of the day, a war film is a paradox - a vehicle of entertainment that also serves a bitter dish of stark reality. It can be seen as a way of discussing the indiscussible, understanding the incomprehensible, or contemplating the unthinkable. Such is the power, the potential, and indeed, the burden of war films.

The chapter ahead will further explore the intricacies of the dialogue around war filmmaking. It is a deep dive into the ethical dimensions of war cinema, guiding us to better understand, appreciate, and create war films that balance artistic expression with sensitivity and truth.

Chapter 10: The Future of War Films

The shift from celluloid reels to digital screens and the dawn of virtual reality have opened new vistas for the war genre. Advanced technologies like CGI and drone cinematography are giving filmmakers the tools to make more realistic and immersive war movies, breaking away from traditional modes of storytelling. The war film genre can't remain shackled to the chronicles of erstwhile wars alone. With the world rapidly changing, new types of conflicts are emerging which are redefining the way we perceive warfare. Civil wars, cyber warfare, and bio-warfare provide fodder for fresh narratives in cinema. Additionally, with global interconnectivity at its peak, the film industry can't ignore the international nature of contemporary conflicts. Ethnic wars, revolutions, and crises in the Middle-East, Africa, and Asia are now becoming part of the global cinematic landscape, bringing various cultures, settings, and even languages to the war genre. This means future war films won't just be about storytelling, but will also help to foster understanding between different cultures impacted by conflict.

Emerging Technologies and Techniques

The art of war film has gained remarkable innovation through the advent of emerging technologies. Filmmakers are continually exploring new frontiers, seeking to immerse their audiences deeper into the heart of combat experiences. Where once viewers observed battles from a safe distance, technology is now allowing them to feel as though they're standing right on the battlefield, immersed in the very action they once reveled from afar.

Leaders in these technological advancements include Virtual Reality (VR) and Augmented Reality (AR). VR fully immerses the viewer in a world detached from reality, while AR enhances the world that the viewer can already see. Ascertaining that realness, immersing the viewer into the throes of war, and allowing them to experience the emotion and tension can attain a greater understanding of a soldier's ordeal. Essentially, VR and AR change the traditional narration style, offering a first-person spectator's perspective.

Moreover, drones are transforming the way war movies are captured. They allow filmmakers to achieve aerial shots that were once impossible or too dangerous to capture. Imagine viewing the grand spectacle of a battlefield from a bird's eye perspective - the troop advancements, the widespread chaos of war. Similarly, Steadicam, a portable stabilizing system, allows for dynamic camera movement, capturing in-the-moment action without jeopardizing camera stability.

Techniques like CGI (Computer Generated Imagery) have proven to be game-changers, further allowing for more realistic depictions of war. With CGI, directors can recreate large-scale battles, weaponry, and aspects of warfare that are too dangerous, too costly, or simply impossible to film. The combination of CGI and Motion Capture technologies can bring scenes to life in a hyper-realistic, safer, and more cost-effective way.

High-dynamic range (HDR) and 4K resolution have significantly enhanced the visual experience. Coupled with superior surround sound systems, they deliver a more realistic and immersive cinematic experience. The viewer now, more than ever, experiences the firepower and the gruesome sounds of war with palpable impact.

Take 3D film technology, for instance, which has turned film viewing into an immersive experience. While the application of 3D technology in war films is still an up-and-coming trend, it's a technique undeniable of its immersive influence. Dramatic camera angles would be utilized to emphasize the depth and perspective of a particular scene, subsequently enhancing the perception of realism.

Profound developments have also taken place in screenwriting techniques. There is a shift from conventional to unconventional narratives, challenging traditional storytelling constructs. For instance, the nonlinear or parallel narrative offers a more complex portrayal of war and its protagonists. Exposing different angles of the same war, contrasting differing human experiences within the same timeframe broadens the narrative scope.

In the editing field, digital technology is reshaping the post-production process. Non-linear editing systems (NLE), for example, allow editors to access any frame in a digital video clip regardless of sequence in the clip. From the final cut to color correction, digital enhancements, and sound design, these advancements give filmmakers greater control to fine-tune their films.

It's also worth observing the rise of digital platforms as an alternative to traditional theatrical releases. Online streaming platforms like Netflix, Amazon Prime, and Hulu have realized the value of war movies and ensure their availability to a global audience. This has not only affected the distribution but also the production of war films as these digital giants are increasingly funding and producing their projects, thus broadening opportunities for innovative filmmakers.

Despite these advancements, the essence of war films remains the same—it's still about telling the untold stories of courage, valor, and human resilience under the worst circumstances. We must keep in mind that technology, in all its grandeur, is but a tool in the hands of a creator, and it's their vision that ultimately transmutes into an articulate piece of work.

The real challenge lies in the careful balance of utilizing these innovations while still maintaining the raw integrity that defines war films. It's about walking that thin line between realistic portrayal and sensationalism, between authenticity and visual spectacle.

The future of war films is more promising than ever. Just picture a war film fully shot in 360 degrees, giving the audiences a wholly immersive experience as never seen before in war cinema. Or imagine witnessing the holographic projection of a war film in your living room, where you're no longer a passive spectator, but an unwitting participant in the unfolding drama. The possibilities are indeed thrilling, the threshold of an adventure unlike any other.

The winds of change are blowing, and they carry with them the promise of a redefined, evolved landscape of war cinema. The allure and fascination of exploring these new avenues are what may breathe new life into this genre that we so dearly cherish. If there's one thing that history of cinema has taught us, it's that the realm of filmmaking is a playground of endless possibilities and constant change. And that, in essence, is the grandeur of cinema and the potent magic it holds over the humankind.

New Conflicts, New Perspectives

As the sun sets on the pinnacles of traditional war films, the dawn of a new era brings fresh perspectives to the silver screen. Cinematic wars have shifted from the battlefields of the World Wars to those of modern conflicts, and with this shift arises a need for diverse viewpoints, innovative stories, and a more nuanced understanding of contemporary warfare. War movies are no longer tied to a specific geographical region or historical event - they now mirror multifaceted international relations, dynamic power structures, and the subjective elements of modern conflict.

In traditional war films, there was often a clear distinction between 'good' and 'evil'. The enemies were evident, and the heroic valor of the soldiers was celebrated. As we move into the era of modern warfare films, these clear-cut delineations become blurred. The lines between heroes and villains are not as definitively drawn, reflecting the complexity and ambiguity of modern day conflicts. There is no longer one side to root for with complete conviction or another to scorn without reservation.

These intricate tales, that examine everyday people caught in the crossfire or the brutal impact of war on innocent civilians, are bringing unique stories to the forefront. Films like 'The Hurt Locker' and 'Zero Dark Thirty' veer away from the battlefield-centric focus of earlier war films and delve into the psychology of soldiers and strategists in uncertain and morally challenging situations.

Filmmakers have recognized the need to explore fresh narratives that reflect the reality of contemporary warfare. Today's conflicts are more about ideologies, political power, and economic supremacy, all of which find representation in films. They handle complex narratives with delicate precision, making them relatable to audiences worldwide. Take the film 'Waltz with Bashir', for instance. The film uses animation to depict the horrors of the Lebanon war and its aftermath in a profound and surreal way, showcasing not only the physical but also the psychological warfare experienced by soldiers.

Filmmakers are also turning their lenses towards unconventional spaces of conflict, from cyber warfare painted in films like 'WarGames' to economic wars depicted in 'The Big Short'. While not traditionally viewed as 'war' films, these movies reflect the broadened understanding of conflict in a globalized and digitized age. Thus, they align with the changing contours of the genre.

The expansion of the genre also indicates an increased representation of varied perspectives. We now see films contemplating the perspectives of women, minorities, and non-combatants alongside that of soldiers. Feminist themes are explored in 'Megan Leavey', and racial inequality is brought to the fore in 'Da 5 Bloods'. Such films allow audiences to gain insight into different experiences and repercussions of war.

The industry's shift has also seen unconventional storytelling methods adopted. Films are breaking away from traditional linear narratives, opting for fragmented or non-linear storytelling that is reflective of the disorienting chaos of war. Additionally, the use of unconventional devices such as subjective camera angles, voice-over narrations, and unreliable narrations allow for a more immersive and intimate cinematic experience.

The access to newer technologies has also helped filmmakers bring their vision to life in ways that were previously impossible. The use of advanced CGI, realistic sound effects, and digital imagery has contributed to creating a more visually stunning and immersive war film experience. Indeed, the sensory overload that these tools enable can often create the illusion of reality, pulling viewers straight onto the battlefield.

Streaming platforms have also played a key role in diversifying the war films genre. They have provided a space for independent filmmakers to experiment with unique narratives and perspectives often overlooked by mainstream cinema. Furthermore, with their global reach, these platforms have internationalized the genre, making it accessible to audiences worldwide, who then understand different cultures and their experiences of war.

Lastly, the film depiction of contemporary warfare has fostered a dialogue on significant issues such as veteran treatment, PTSD, and civilian casualties. By sensitively handling these narratives, the stigma attached to such conversations is reduced, promoting a broader understanding and empathy among viewers.

The myriad of narrative structures, thematic explorations, and visual innovations mark the genre's evolution. War films have been reinvented to mirror the changing face of conflicts in the modern era, opening up a plethora of perspectives previously unconsidered.

War films are a vibrant and evolving art form that continues to entrall audiences with gripping narratives, intense performances, and innovative filmmaking techniques. As we look towards the future, we can't wait to see how this genre will continue to chronicle the times, document our history, and shape societal attitudes towards warfare. It's not just about entertaining audiences, but about opening their eyes to new perspectives and realities, offering a window into the raw and hallowed corners of human existence.

Through the lens of the filmmaker, we are witnesses to the unfolding narrative of human conflict, drawn into the intricate tapestry of heroism, sacrifice, and resilience. As we delve deeper into the world of war films, we continue to discover new conflicts but also, critically, new viewpoints. These cinematic narratives not only recount stories of the bygone past but also probe into the heart of contemporary society, daring to question, challenge and inspire.

Stay tuned, for the world of war films offers a never-ending exploration of human courage and despair, hope and resignation, justice and morality. Let's turn the page and unravel the poignant and powerful exploration of cinemas' frontline as we look back at this remarkable journey and anticipate the exciting future that lies ahead.

The Globalization of War Cinema

The globalization of war cinema is a phenomenon that mirrors the changing dynamics of warfare itself. Just as the settings and players on the world's battlefields have shifted and diversified, so too have the voices and perspectives in war cinema. As both a response to and an influencer of these changes, global war cinema has grown to cover broader narratives, taking on an increasingly international scope with such progression being rooted in technological, economical, and cultural evolution.

Hithertofore, war films were essentially dominated by a limited number of heavily involved nations such as the United States and the United Kingdom. These powerful nations trailed a blaze, setting the benchmarks of narratives, themes, and perspectives that constituted the genre of war cinema. It wasn't until the rise of globalization that the restrictions began to thaw, giving birth to a more diversified ensemble of voices in this genre.

As film technology and distribution channels expanded globally, so too did the ability for stories to be told from a multitude of perspectives. This opened the door to a broader range of war narratives, many of which notably diverged from the well-trodden, traditional views of the genre. It revealed the potential for war cinema to become a platform for exploring untold stories, bringing hitherto ignored experiences to light, and challenging dominant narratives.

Languages other than English started to emerge on the soundscape of war films—from the picturesque French in "Indigènes" to the haunting Khmer in "The Killing Fields." These films challenged the traditional perspectives presented in war cinema by offering intricate narrative viewpoints that strayed away from the mainstream. The use of native languages alone further nuanced the authenticity of the representation, increasing the emotional intensity and realism of the films.

The progression of war narratives towards global themes has been gradual and not without its hindrances. Co-productions between countries, for instance, have often been prove challenging, raising issues of creative control, funding, and distribution. Nevertheless, they've provided an invaluable avenue for cross-cultural collaboration and understanding, challenging the genre's entrenched habitual perspectives.

The global democratization of film distribution platforms such as streaming services has become a powerful engine propelling this globalization. No longer bound by conventional distribution models, filmmakers can now directly connect with worldwide audiences, increasing the visibility of underrepresented voices. It's a reciprocal process where audiences keen on diverse narratives encourage creators from both familiar and unfamiliar terrains of war to visualize their narrative and perspective.

By melding multiple cultural lenses, global war cinema provides a richer, multifaceted portrayal of the horrors, heroisms, and humanities misunderstood or oversimplified in traditional war narratives. It excels in breaking stereotypes and peels back the layers of cultural understanding, inviting the audience to reconsider their knowledge and beliefs about war.

Furthermore, the geographical widening of war cinema comes a diversification and complication of the concept of war itself. The genre is no longer confined to large-scale conflicts between nations. Movies like "City of God" and "Beasts of No Nation", for instance, illustrate the devastations of civil war and gang wars in a nationally bounded frame.

Yet, as we navigate the unchartered territory brought about by the globalization of war cinema, we must bear the responsibility to accurately and respectably represent cultures besides our own. The fervor for diversity and universality should never give way to misinterpretation, over-simplification, or exploitation of different cultures and histories. Filmmakers ought to contemplate and uphold the fine balance of sharing and respecting varied cultures' narratives.

Moreover, with a wider range of countries now contributing to the narrative of war on film, we see a much more diversified and complex portrayal of military strategy, combat techniques and warfare technology. This not only expanded our understanding but also question our preexisting notions of these aspects.

While global war cinema encourages fresh perspectives, it nevertheless remains susceptible to repeating the pitfalls of the past. It is a delicate tightrope to walk, balancing the need for authenticity and diversity with the risk of perpetuating war cinema's historically harmful hierarchies and sensationalism.

Understanding the globalization of war cinema is to appreciate the interplay of differing cultures, philosophies of filmmaking, and evolving technology. It's about recognizing the shared threads and divergent strands that compose the multifaceted tapestry of the genre. Far from being a threat to war cinema, globalization is an enriching force, one that encourages a myriad of voices and experiences, fostering a more comprehensive and profound understanding of war and its aftermath.

Ultimately, the essence of the globalization of war cinema is its ability to offer nuanced representations of struggles, victories, and traumas that are understated, overlooked, or misunderstood in mainstream war films. After all, at the heart of war cinema, beyond all battles and glory, lies the universally shared human experiences—of trauma, struggling, victory, and loss. As we navigate this ever-globalized world, may we continue to use war cinema as a lens through which to understand, empathize, and learn from each other's experiences, and perhaps, to ultimately inspire a more peaceful world.

As we ponder the future of war films, it's clear that the genre's destiny is intertwined with the paths of war themselves. As global tensions take on new shapes and forms — from cyber warfare to proxy wars — it seems inevitable that war cinema will follow suit, consistently evolving, mirroring, and reacting to our ever-globalizing, ever-changing world.

116

Chapter 11: Reflecting on Cinema's Frontline

We must take a moment, now, to look back on the long and storied journey of war films, from their humble, silent beginnings to the thunderous, technologically advanced spectacles of today. These films, much like the conflicts they represent, have left an indelible mark on society, shaping and being shaped by the zeitgeist. They function, in essence, as a mirror, reflecting the values, hopes, fears, and realities of their time. But this mirror is not merely passive; it can also spark change, initiating dialogues that reshape our collective understanding. War films, therefore, occupy a unique intersection between art and reality — not merely mimicking the world but actively partaking in its evolution. The ongoing impact and legacy of these films are monumental, not only in the realm of cinema but also in the annals of social and political discourse. They have become so intertwined with our perception and memory of wars that, in some cases, they have silently supplanted the raw experiences, fostering a collective pictorial memory. The lines between fiction and reality blur in the most immersive ensembles of our century, creating a frontline battlefield that lies not just in the trenches of some distant land, but in every theater, every living room where a war film unfurls its potent narrative.

A Look Back at the Journey

There's something of profound significance in war films, with their potent blend of entertainment and enlightenment. War films have long been a mirror for society, reflecting the world's tumultuous state, and in many cases, highlighting paths towards change. As we glance over our shoulder on the long road this fascinating genre has taken, we cannot help but recognize the brave pioneers who dared to undertake this demanding and often controversial task.

The birth of this genre saw cinema used as a battlefield itself, swiftly transitioning from a form of escapism to a platform where nations waged cultural war. The silent era was instrumental in setting the foundation, using innovative techniques to narrate stories of war without uttering a word. These early interpretations were resplendent in their simplicity and their raw, unfiltered depictions of the harsh realities of war.

In the Golden Age of Hollywood, the lens of the camera focused on World War II, crafting both art and propaganda. World War II welcomed an avalanche of films that did more than portray war; they painted vivid pictures of patriotism, courage, and the indomitable human spirit. This era also witnessed the cinema's potential ripple effect on society, long after the dust of war had settled.

The advent of the Cold War shifted war films to more obscure territory, reflecting the invisible nature of the conflict. With the aid of cinematic foresight, filmmakers during this era skillfully depicted the cultural anxieties of their time, boldly resonating with their not-so-distant reality.

And then came the Vietnam War, infamously etched in history and the silver screen for its vivid portrayal of carnage. War films suddenly strayed from mere entertainment or propaganda, inspiring instead a strong sense of realism and raw emotion. Filmmakers weaponized cinema to voice their disdain, spurring influential waves of protest across the nation.

With the onset of the technological age and modern warfare, war films have undergone a drastic metamorphosis, bringing innovative approaches to the genre. Fueled by these advancements, the portrayal of war and conflict took a different hue, reflecting society's evolving viewpoints on such grave matters.

In tandem with society's shifting tides, war films also began focusing their lens on the veterans themselves, underscoring the immense impact wars had on these brave souls. Through cinematic representation, examination of trauma, and the inclusion of veterans in film production, filmmakers successfully unmasked the cost of war, humanizing those who were once dehumanized.

As the genre progressed, war films started acknowledging the crucial roles of women and minorities in wars, shattering long-standing stereotypes. Breakthrough films and characters compelled audiences to question and reevaluate their perceptions, using cinema as a vehicle for social commentary.

Running alongside these developments were the ethical considerations in war filmmaking. Striking a balance between art and sensitivity, filmmakers negotiated their way through numerous controversies and criticisms, giving birth to numerous ethical debates and discussions within the industry.

Fast forward to the future, we see the genre still in flux, dictated by emerging technologies, global perspectives, and new conflicts. War films have become less defined by boundaries as they take on a more global outlook. Moreover, the advancement of technologies is changing the way war stories are told.

Looking back at the path war films have charted, the journey is as intricate as it's enlightening. Yet, through its highs and lows, the genre's ongoing impact and legacy remain a testament to the art's power and resilience. In spite of the many difficulties, criticisms, and the inherent grimness of its subject matter, war films have never shied away from challenging norms and pushing cinematic boundaries.

As we reach the end of our retrospective exploration, we cannot help but admire the power of the genre. War movies, throughout their evolution, have demonstrated the truly monumental effect of cinema on society. They have brought humanity closer to realities often distant and foreign, stirred empathy, and sparked important discussions around war and its aftermath.

This journey is far from over, however. The genre is destined for even more significant revolutions, each carrying with it the potential to change perceptions and social narratives. It's in stark contradictions, the intersection of art and reality, that war cinema truly leaves a lasting imprint on its audience and society at large.

So here we are, having taken a step back to see the journey. We have seen where we started, where we've been, and can only dream about where we might go next. This genre, vibrant and resilient, will continue to chronicle stories of war, conflict, and humanity. And as it evolves, we can be sure it will continue to challenge us, move us, and foster essential conversations about our world and our place in it.

Ongoing Impact and Legacy

As we look to the horizon, cast our eyes broad and far, one can't help but admit the palpable impact of war films on our perceptions of battles past and present. The celluloid chronicles of human conflicts carry on resonating long after their credit rolls have passed, their celluloid battles echoing our collective consciousness.

From the courageous soldiers storming the beaches of Normandy in 'Saving Private Ryan,' to the terrified young men trapped by enemy fire in 'Full Metal Jacket,' war films have shaped our understanding of wars considerably. Just as wars have left indelible marks on our society and psyche, so too have their on-screen depictions. These films have sculpted our collective memory and molded public sentiment about these momentous and tragic events.

Observe as an example the perceptible rise in patriotism during the post-World War II era. The depictions of heroic acts, bravery, and sacrifices made during the war in films of the Golden Age were instrumental in fostering a profound sense of national pride. Without them, our morale might have waned in the wake of such a cataclysmic struggle.

In the throes of the Cold War, cinematic expressions reflected an age of suspicion and fear. Movies from this era, like 'Dr. Strangelove' or 'Fail Safe,' became mirrors of societal anxiety towards nuclear armageddon, pervading our cultural fabric. These films served to cement and amplify our collective anxieties about the horrifying consequences of nuclear warfare.

We can't overlook the impact of Vietnam War films either. The raw, unfiltered narratives of films like 'Apocalypse Now' and 'The Deer Hunter' presented a stark contrast to the supposedly righteous and patriotic wartime tales of yore. They disassembled the romanticized image of war, revealing the harrowing truths, and in doing so, radically changed our perspective towards war, its consequences, and those who partake in them.

Whenever new forms of warfare rise, you'll find the cinema's lens pointed steadily at them, recording, analyzing, and reflecting through the medium of film. Modern warfare, with its drone strikes and cyber attacks, are ripe themes for contemporary war cinema, telling tales of their unique terrors and quandaries.

The indomitable presence of war films has not just touched audiences but played a crucial role in helping veterans process their experiences. Films often serve as therapeutic tools for those disturbed by the horrors of war, helping them come to terms with their trauma. For many who've served, these films often provide an invaluable outlet where words fail to describe their experiences.

War films have been instrumental in driving social change, too – particularly in the representation of women and minorities. These cinematic sagas have evolved from their early days of excluding or marginalizing these groups, steadily shifting towards more inclusive, accurate portrayals. This seismic shift in representation is, in itself, a testimony to the power and influence of war films.

A discussion of the legacy of war films would be incomplete without a nod to the ongoing ethical debate surrounding the consequences of war filmmaking. The battle between artistic freedom, sensitivity toward the subject matter, and responsibility towards accurate portrayal perpetuates in filmmaking. This tension continually shapes the narrative of war films, leading to its ever-evolving legacy.

Looking forward, emerging technologies and new narrative techniques promise to keep the genre vibrant and instrumental in shaping our perceptions of conflict. We stand at an exciting crossroad of virtual reality, immersive storytelling, and global perspectives, all poised to redefine war cinema's legacy.

Nevertheless, as global as cinema may be, wars being fought in disparate parts of the world will always lend unique, vivid hues to on-screen warfare, allowing us to empathize with diverse experiences of conflict, resistance, and survival - pushing the reach of war movies beyond specific regions.

Indeed, war films have transcended their mere cinematic boundaries and secured a firm seat at the table where art and reality intersect. They've assumed the mantle of storytellers, educators, chroniclers, and provocateurs, constantly challenging us to reevaluate our views on war, its heroes, villains, victims, and survivors.

In the final reckoning, the ongoing impact and legacy of war films is an intricate web, woven with threads of societal evolution, technological progress, human conflict, and cinematic innovation. They're mirrors we hold up to explore our past, understand our present, and foresee our future conflicts.

So as we reflect upon these moving pictures of strife and valor, let us remember that war films are far more than just cinema - they're a testament to our human capacity to endure, to fight, to change, and above all, to remember.

The Intersection of Art and Reality

As we delve into the final chapter, the enticing world of war cinema beckons us into its depth, where art and reality mingle in a unique dance of creativity and truth. Even though these films walk the line between factual and fictional, there's an uncanny allure in the magic of their craft. Bear witness as cinema spins tales of valor and bravery, mired in the brutal truth of human warfare.

In essence, war films strive to maintain a delicate balance - they're bound by the duty to mirror the grim realities of war, yet they can't forsake their creative liberties. As viewers, we get caught in this crossfire of authenticity and imagination, compelling us to gaze deeper into the crux of real-world conflicts.

How do directors achieve this blend of realism and drama? More often than not, they lean upon historical battles as their source material. They weave a cinematic narrative through the threads of true events, casting a prism over our perspectives of bygone eras. These films transport us to the heart of combat zones, where we silently grapple with its harsh truths.

Nevertheless, there's an undeniable artistry involved in this process, as each director uses a unique lens to view these events. This is where their storytelling prowess shines, turning Achilles into actors and battlegrounds into sets, while gracefully navigating the minefield of historical integrity.

No war film is an objective document, untouched by the filmmaker's vision. Every flicker on the screen is a reflection of directorial choices, vastly influenced by an individual or collective ideology. It's this narrative, carefully intertwined with factual events, that defines the film's imprint on viewers and society alike.

Art, in this context, isn't merely an aesthetic consideration but a means of guiding viewers towards a deeper understanding of war. It's not just the visuals that matter, it's the director's ability to encapsulate the entire spectrum of human experience in a few frames. It's this semblance of art that helps us relate with the characters, oftentimes helping us register the unfathomable repercussions of war.

Reality in war films isn't a mere canvas for a director's creative impulses. The real-life implications of their work necessitate a sense of responsibility in them. They need to respect the war narrative and the people involved - be it victims, heroes, or villains. Straying too far into fictional territory, may lead to a disservice not only to the art but to history too.

The challenge here lies in straddling the thin line between creative story-telling and factual representation—packageName packs as much intensity into a war movie. The reality being the eventful backdrop against which art blossoms in its full grandeur. Yet, with every stroke of creativity, the artist must tread carefully, respectful of the gravity of the scenes they are illustrating.

The shared goal of these films—beyond entertainment—is manifest; to evoke emotional reactions, provoke thought, and often to memorialize historical events. Yet it's the haunting blend of art and reality that makes them a genre apart, at once troubling and fascinating.

Thus, the intersection of art and reality in war films explores the fascinating confluence of creativity and authenticity, where each complements the other. It's a quest to bring forth the harrowing truth of armed conflict in a manner that captivates the viewer, while maintaining reverence for historical accuracy.

This intersection isn't a crossroads where the two paths meet and part ways. Instead, it's a junction where art and reality orbit around each other in a ceaseless exchange. Art brings war to life, while reality grounds art in historical significance. It's a symbiotic relationship that impacts viewers on varying levels.

Filmmakers, like soldiers, take great risks when plunging into the field of war cinema. They shoulder the burden of truth, endeavoring to relay stories that resonate deeply within the audience. The ultimate goal is to project the stark reality of war through artistic hallucination—to portray the atrocity, honor, suffering, and inevitability that war invariably engenders.

All said and done, the intersection of art and reality forms the critical core of war cinema. It's where memories, history, and trauma coalesce to narrate a tale of monumental trials and tribulations. Whether representing the tremendous heroism of soldiers or the poignant plight of innocents caught in the crossfire, these films capture the essence of war's dual visage – stark and theatrical.

They say that art imitates life—war films are a testament to this. They offer us a glimpse into the grim realities of war, painstakingly painted on the canvas of cinema. By merging art with reality, they champion a new realm of storytelling—one that ventures deep into the heart of human conflict and emerges triumphant, bearing tales of unseen valor and undying spirit.